Fresh Illustrations
for Preaching
and Teaching

Fresh Illustrations for Preaching and Teaching

From Leadership Journal

Edited by
Edward K. Rowell

Baker Books

A Division of Baker Book House Co
Grand Rapids, Michigan 49516

Copublished by Christianity Today, Inc., and Baker Books
a division of Baker Book House Company
P.O. Box 6287, Grand Rapids, MI 49516-6287

Second printing, September 1998

Printed in the United States of America

Library of Congress Cataloging-in-Publication Data

Fresh illustrations for preaching and teaching : from Leadership journal / edited by Edward K. Rowell.
      p. cm.
   Includes index.
   ISBN 0-8010-9048-2 (cloth)
    1. Homiletical illustrations. I. Rowell, Edward K. II. Leadership (Carol Stream, Ill.)
   BV4225.2F73 1997
   251'.08—dc21   97-30785

For information about academic books, resources for Christian leaders, and all new releases available from Baker Book House, visit our web site: http://www.bakerbooks.com

Introduction

I was sitting with a bunch of magazine editors recently, listening to Sharon Grigsby, editor of the award-winning religion section of the *Dallas Morning News*. She was encouraging us to focus our magazines, not on the issues editors care about, rather on the issues *readers* care about. She told a story to make her point.

The editors of the *Dallas Morning News* "Foods" section love exotic recipes requiring rare ingredients, high levels of culinary skill, and hours of preparation and presentation. Though the editors win awards for photography and journalism, many of their page-one selections are out of the reach of most cooks.

These food editors were shocked when a reader survey revealed that the highest-rated article of the past year had been a short, non-feature piece on "What to Do with Stale Bread."

Grigsby concluded: "Whatever else you provide for your readers, be sure and tell them how to use their stale bread."

Her skillful use of a simple story introduced a new term into our vocabulary. When I talked recently with another editor from that conference, she told me about the forthcoming "stale bread" story in her magazine. A simple story helps her remember to ask how she can serve her reader's daily, practical needs.

We preachers often lament that people forget our carefully crafted exposition and remember our simple stories. I contend that's not a problem—if we tell the right stories.

Fresh Illustrations for Preaching and Teaching offers you a storehouse of powerful, contemporary stories that will cause your listeners to remember your next sermon or talk.

To make this preaching resource even more useful and time saving, we provide:

1. *The right to copy.* You have the right to copy these illustrations and file them in the way that best fits your system.

2. *Topical arrangement.* We've filed each illustration under the topics that come to mind during sermon study. You'll find fresh material for your next sermon on Anger, Salvation, or Worship.

3. *Alternate subjects and index.* Each illustration is followed by two alternate subjects in parentheses. Since any good story has more than one application, you can find the reference you need indexed under at least three topics.

Give these simple stories a try. And while you're at it, why not preach a "stale bread" sermon next Sunday?

—*Ed Rowell*
Editor, PREACHING TODAY
Assistant Editor, LEADERSHIP JOURNAL
Carol Stream, Illinois

A university professor tells of being invited to speak at a military base one December and there meeting an unforgettable soldier named Ralph. Ralph had been sent to meet him at the airport. After they had introduced themselves, they headed toward the baggage claim.

As they walked down the concourse, Ralph kept disappearing. Once to help an older woman whose suitcase had fallen open. Once to lift two toddlers up to where they could see Santa Claus, again to give directions to someone who was lost. Each time he came back with a smile on his face.

"Where did you learn that?" the professor asked.

"What?" Ralph said.

"Where did you learn to live like that?"

"Oh," Ralph said, "during the war, I guess." He then told the professor about his tour of duty in Vietnam, how it was his job to clear mine fields, how he watched his friends blow up before his eyes, one after another.

"I learned to live between steps," he said. "I never knew whether the next one would be my last, so I learned to get everything I could out of the moment between when I picked up my foot and when I put it down again. Every step I took was a whole new world, and I guess I've been that way ever since."

The abundance of our lives is not determined by how long we live, but by how well we live.

—Barbara Brown Taylor
(Fulfillment, Serving)

Dates used:_____

Acceptance

In *The Whisper Test*, Mary Ann Bird writes:

I grew up knowing I was different, and I hated it. I was born with a cleft palate, and when I started school, my classmates made it clear to me how I looked to others: a little girl with a misshapen lip, crooked nose, lopsided teeth, and garbled speech.

When schoolmates asked, "What happened to your lip?" I'd tell them I'd fallen and cut it on a piece of glass. Somehow it seemed more acceptable to have suffered an accident than to have been born different. I was convinced that no one outside my family could love me.

There was, however, a teacher in the second grade whom we all adored—Mrs. Leonard. She was short, round, happy—a sparkling lady.

Annually we had a hearing test. . . . Mrs. Leonard gave the test to everyone in the class, and finally it was my turn. I knew from past years that as we stood against the door and covered one ear, the teacher sitting at her desk would whisper something, and we would have to repeat it back—things like "The sky is blue" or "Do you have new shoes?" I waited there for those words that God must have put into her mouth, those seven words that changed my life. Mrs. Leonard said, in her whisper, "I wish you were my little girl."

God says to every person deformed by sin, "I wish you were my son" or "I wish you were my daughter."

(Encouragement, Love)

Dates used:_____

Jawanza Kunjufu, in his book, *Restoring the Village,* writes:

When I was a 14-year-old high school freshman, school was dismissed early for a teachers' meeting. I conveniently neglected to tell my parents about the change and arranged to bring my girlfriend over to my house. We weren't planning to study.

As we were going up the steps, my neighbor, Mrs. Nolan, poked her head out of a window and said, "You're home awfully early, Jerome."

"Yes, Ma'am," I said, improvising a lame story about how we planned to review algebra problems.

"Does your mother know you're home this early," Mrs. Nolan persisted, "and do you want me to call her?"

I gave up. "No, Ma'am. I'll go inside and call her while Kathy sits on the porch."

Mrs. Nolan saved our careers that day. If Kathy had gotten pregnant, she might not have become the doctor she is today. And my father had warned me that if I made a baby, the mutual fund he set up for me to go to college or start a business would have gone to the child. I'm glad Mrs. Nolan was at her window, looking out for me.

(Abstinence, Neighbors)

Dates used:_____

Accountability

On February 26, 1995, Barings, the oldest bank in Britain, announced it was seeking bankruptcy protection after losing nearly one billion dollars in a stock gamble, according to *Time* magazine.

In late 1994, the chief trader at Barings's Singapore office began betting big on Japan's Nikkei market. Then disaster struck. An earthquake hit Kobe, Japan, and on January 23, 1995, the Nikkei plunged more than one thousand points.

Barings Bank lost big money. But instead of cutting his losses, Barings's Singapore trader doubled his investment, apparently hoping that the Nikkei would rebound. It didn't. Barings's London office put up nearly $900 million to support its falling position on the Singapore investments. Finally, Barings ran out of capital and declared bankruptcy.

How could one twenty-eight-year-old trader in Singapore lose nearly a billion dollars and ruin a 233-year-old British bank? According to *Time,* the problem was lack of supervision.

"London allowed [the Singapore trader] to take control of both the trading desk and the backroom settlement operation in Singapore. It is a mix that can be—and in this case was—toxic. . . . A trader keeping his own books is like a schoolboy grading his own tests; the temptation to cheat can be overwhelming, particularly if the stakes are high enough."

—Craig Brian Larson
Contemporary Illustrations for Preachers, Teachers, and Writers
(Risk, Temptation)

Dates used:_____

In a 1994 article, "Wars' Lethal Leftovers Threaten Europeans," Associated Press reporter Christopher Burns writes:

The bombs of World War II are still killing in Europe. They turn up—and sometimes blow up—at construction sites, in fishing nets, or on beaches fifty years after the guns fell silent.

Hundreds of tons of explosives are recovered every year in France alone. Thirteen old bombs exploded in France in 1993, killing twelve people and wounding eleven.

"I've lost two of my colleagues," said Yvon Bouvet, who heads a government team in the Champagne-Ardennes region that defuses explosives from both World War I and II. "Unexploded bombs become more dangerous with time. With the corrosion inside, the weapon becomes more unstable, and the detonator can be exposed."

What is true of lingering bombs is also true of lingering anger. Buried anger will explode when we least expect it.

—Barry McGee
(Resentment, Temper)

Dates used:_____

Anger

In his autobiography, *Number 1,* Billy Martin told about hunting in Texas with Mickey Mantle. Mickey had a friend who would let them hunt on his ranch. When they reached the ranch, Mickey told Billy to wait in the car while he checked in with his friend.

Mantle's friend quickly gave them permission to hunt, but he asked Mickey a favor. He had a pet mule in the barn who was going blind, and didn't have the heart to put him out of his misery. He asked Mickey to shoot the mule for him.

When Mickey came back to the car, he pretended to be angry. He scowled and slammed the door. Billy asked him what was wrong, and Mickey said his friend wouldn't let them hunt. "I'm so mad at that guy," Mantle said, "I'm going out to his barn and shoot one of his mules!"

Martin protested, "We can't do that!"

But Mickey was adamant. "Just watch me."

He jumped out of the car with his rifle, ran inside the barn, and shot the mule. As he was leaving, though, he heard two shots. He saw that Martin had taken out his rifle, too.

"What are you doing, Martin?" he yelled.

Martin yelled back, face red with anger, "We'll show that son of a gun! I just killed two of his cows!"

Anger can be dangerously contagious. As Proverbs puts it, "Do not make friends with a hot-tempered man ... or you may learn his ways" (Prov. 22:24–25).

—Scott Bowerman
(Rage, Relationships)

Dates used:_____

The *Arizona Republic* (4/25/95) reported that when Steve Tran of Westminster, California, closed the door on twenty-five activated bug bombs, he thought he had seen the last of the cockroaches that shared his apartment. When the spray reached the pilot light of the stove, it ignited, blasting his screen door across the street, breaking all his windows, and setting his furniture ablaze.

"I really wanted to kill all of them," he said. "I thought if I used a lot more, it would last longer." According to the label, just two canisters of the fumigant would have solved Tran's roach problem.

The blast caused over $10,000 damage to the apartment building. And the cockroaches? Tran reported, "By Sunday, I saw them walking around."

As Proverbs 29:11 says, only "a fool gives full vent to his anger."

(Foolishness, Overkill)

Dates used:_____

Assisted Suicide

A lva B. Weir, an oncologist in Germantown, Tennessee, told this true story:

I was awakened from sleep by the telephone. On the other end of the line, a distraught woman told me that her son, a cancer patient of one of my partners, was unconscious, breathing badly, with an empy bottle of pills at his bedside. I inquired further and learned this patient had recently discovered that his cancer had metastasized to his bone.

Along with his pain, he had lost control of his bowels. He could not tolerate the thought of pain and incontinence with no hope of cure. He had decided to end his life and appeared close to succeeding.

The mother did not know what to do. I convinced her to bring him to the hospital where we could evaluate him.

I met them in the emergency room. The mother, brother, and sister were there. The patient was breathing badly and looked as if he were dying from the overdose. I examined the patient, checked the laboratory results, and recommended that we lavage his stomach and place him on a ventilator until the drugs left his system.

The mother was uncertain; the brother took charge, suggesting that the patient desired suicide and that they should honor his wishes and let him die in peace rather than bring him through to face life with cancer. They insisted on taking him home with no therapy.

I worked with them for some time, and they compromised by allowing me to admit him to the hospital with only oxygen and intravenous fluid support, but no tubes and no ventilator. They consented mainly because of logistical and legal complications produced by a patient dying at home of suicide.

I admitted him, expecting him to die. His care was resumed by his physician, my partner. The following weekend I was rounding for my group and was surprised to find this patient's name on my list. I walked into the room to find a beaming mother and an alert patient. With the minimal support, he had survived his overdose. After another week, he was walking with his pain improved, bowels controlled, and depression diminished.

I realized that this man and his family, who had chosen for him the absence of life forever, were experiencing precious moments together of unfathomable value. . . . There is no one this side of heaven who has the ability to make the correct decision regarding when our life should be extinguished.

—*Today's Christian Doctor* (Spring 1997)
(Death, Life)

Dates used:_____

Blood of Christ

J effrey Ebert shares this story:

When I was five years old, before factory-installed seat belts and automobile air bags, my family was driving home at night on a two-lane country road. I was sitting on my mother's lap when another car, driven by a drunk driver, swerved into our lane and hit us head-on. I don't have any memory of the collision. I do recall the fear and confusion I felt as I saw myself literally covered with blood from head to toe.

Then I learned that the blood wasn't mine at all, but my mother's. In that split second when the two headlights glared into her eyes, she instinctively pulled me closer to her chest and curled her body around mine. It was her body that slammed against the dashboard, her head that shattered the windshield. She took the impact of the collision so that I wouldn't have to. It took extensive surgery for my mother to recover from her injuries.

In a similar, but infinitely more significant way, Jesus Christ took the impact for our sin, and his blood now permanently covers our lives.

(Atonement, Sacrifice)

Dates used:_____

A few years ago, Alex Dovales was drifting to Miami on a rickety boat with twenty-seven other Cubans. A year later, he was an angel.

Fourteen exhausted and penniless Cuban rafters washed ashore on Key Largo. The rafters had spent four days huddled in an eighteen-foot raft with little water and a few rusted cans filled with meat. Dovales looked at them—"and felt like I had just arrived here myself."

The 25-year-old, who clears $197 per week as a dishwasher, walked home and gathered all the presents from under his Christmas tree. He gave the gifts—each containing shirts and other clothing—to the new arrivals. "They were wet and cold," said Henry Paez, Dovales's roommate. "Alex took off his shirt and gave it to them."

Dovales said he didn't give it a second thought. "They had nothing," he said.

—*Telegraph Herald*
(Empathy, Generosity)

Dates used:_____

Church

In Hot Springs, Arkansas, you'll find the Morris Antique Mall. Nothing on the inside distinguishes this antique store from dozens like it in town. There's a musty smell and dusty relics from the past.

But if you look closely at the outside of the Morris Antique Mall, you'll see something that makes it distinct: before it was an antique store, it was a church building.

A focus on the future prevents a church from becoming a resting place for dusty relics.

—Michael A. Howe
(Future, Vision)

Dates used:_____

In *Living Above the Level of Mediocrity,* Chuck Swindoll writes:

On Sunday, believers arrived at a house church in the Soviet Union in small groups throughout the day so not to arouse the suspicion of KGB informers. They began by singing a hymn quietly. Suddenly, in walked two soldiers with loaded weapons at the ready. One shouted, "If you wish to renounce your commitment to Jesus Christ, leave now!"

Two or three quickly left, then another. After a few more seconds, two more.

"This is your last chance. Either turn against your faith in Christ," he ordered, "or stay and suffer the consequences."

Two more slipped out into the night. No one else moved. Parents with children trembling beside them looked down reassuringly, fully expecting to be gunned down or imprisoned.

The other soldier closed the door, looked back at those who stood against the wall and said, "Keep your hands up—but this time in praise to our Lord Jesus Christ. We, too, are Christians. We were sent to another house church several weeks ago to arrest a group of believers…"

The other soldier interrupted, "But, instead, we were converted! We have learned by experience, however, that unless people are willing to die for their faith, they cannot be fully trusted."

—David Waggoner
(Faith, Trust)

Dates used:_____

Communion

Henri J. M. Nouwen writes in the March 1994 *New Oxford Review:*

A few years ago Bob, the husband of a friend of mine, died suddenly of a heart attack. My friend decided to keep her two young children away from the funeral. She thought it would be too hard for them to see their father put in the ground. For years after Bob's death, the cemetery remained a fearful and a dangerous place for them.

One day, my friend asked me to visit the grave with her, and invited the children to come along. The elder one was too afraid to go, but the younger one decided to come with us. When we came to the place where Bob was buried, the three of us sat down on the grass around the stone engraved with the words, A KIND AND GENTLE MAN.

I said: "Maybe one day we should have a picnic here. This is not only a place to think about death, but also a place to rejoice in our life. Bob will be most honored when we find new strength, here, to live."

At first it seemed a strange idea: having a meal on top of a tombstone. But isn't that similar to what Jesus told his disciples to do when he asked them to share bread and wine in his memory?

A few days later my friend took her elder child to the grave, the younger one having convinced his sister that there was nothing to fear. Now they often go to the cemetery and tell each other stories about Bob.

(Celebration, Resurrection)

Dates used:_____

A few winters ago, heavy snows hit North Carolina. Following a wet, six-inch snowfall, it was interesting to see the effect along Interstate 40.

Next to the highway stood several large groves of tall, young pine trees. The branches were bowed down with the heavy snow—so low that branches from one tree were often leaning against the trunk or branches of another.

Where trees stood alone, however, the effect of the heavy snow was different. The branches had become heavier, but without other trees to lean against, the branches snapped. They lay on the ground, dark and alone in the cold snow.

When the storms of life hit, we need to be standing close to other Christians. The closer we stand, the more we will be able to hold up.

—Carl G. Conner
(Fellowship, Support)

Dates used:_____

Compassion

A student asked anthropologist Margaret Mead for the earliest sign of civilization in a given culture. He expected the answer to be a clay pot or perhaps a fish hook or grinding stone.

Her answer was: "A healed femur."

Mead explained that no mended bones are found where the law of the jungle, survival of the fittest, reigns. A healed femur shows that someone cared. Someone had to do that injured person's hunting and gathering until the leg healed. The evidence of compassion is the first sign of civilization.

—R. Wayne Willis
(Caring, Civilization)

Dates used:_____

On Monday, August 9, 1993, a 31-year-old woman, Sophia White, burst into the hospital nursery at UCLA Medical Center in Los Angeles, wielding a .38-caliber handgun. She had come gunning for Elizabeth Staten, a nurse whom she accused of stealing her husband. White fired six shots, hitting Staten in the wrist and stomach.

Staten fled, and White chased her into the emergency room, firing once more. There, with blood on her clothes and a hot pistol in her hand, the attacker was met by another nurse, Joan Black, who did the unthinkable. Black walked calmly to the gun-toting woman, hugged her and spoke comforting words.

The assailant said she didn't have anything to live for, that Staten had stolen her family.

"You're in pain," Black said. "I'm sorry, but everybody has pain in their lives. . . . I understand, and we can work it out."

As they talked, the hospital invader kept her finger on the trigger. Once she began to lift the gun as if to shoot herself. Nurse Black just pushed her arm down and continued to hold her. At last Sophia White gave the gun to the nurse.

She was disarmed by a hug. It's amazing what compassion can do.

—Tom Tripp
(Courage, Empathy)

Dates used:_____

Compassion

In 1975 a child named Raymond Dunn, Jr., was born in New York State. The Associated Press reports that at his birth, a skull fracture and oxygen deprivation caused severe retardation. As Raymond grew, the family discovered further impairments. His twisted body suffered up to twenty seizures per day. He was blind, mute, immobile. He had severe allergies that limited him to only one food: a meat-based formula made by Gerber Foods.

In 1985, Gerber stopped making the formula that Raymond lived on. His mother scoured the country to buy what stores had in stock, accumulating cases and cases, but in 1990 her supply ran out. In desperation, she appealed to Gerber for help. Without this particular food, Raymond would starve to death.

The employees of the company listened. In an unprecedented action, volunteers donated hundreds of hours to bring out old equipment, set up production lines, obtain special approval from the USDA, and produce the formula—all for one special boy.

In January 1995, Raymond Dunn, Jr., known as the Gerber Boy, died from his physical problems. But during his brief lifetime he called forth a wonderful thing called compassion.

—Larry A. Payne
(Service, Teamwork)

Dates used:_____

In January 1697, on a fast day called to remember the Salem witch trials, Samuel Sewall slipped a document into the hands of his pastor, Samuel Willard, at Boston's Old South Meeting House.

Sewall, one of the seven judges who had sentenced twenty people to death in Salem five years earlier, stood silent before the congregation as Willard read: "Samuel Sewall, sensible of the reiterated strokes of God upon himself and family . . . desires to take the blame and shame of it, asking pardon of men, and especially desiring prayers that God, who has an unlimited authority, would pardon that sin and his other sins. . . .

Sewall believed that eleven of his fourteen children had died as divine punishment for his involvement in the witch trials. His only spiritual hope was confession as public as his sin.

—*Yankee* (1/97)
(Repentance, Responsibility)

Dates used:_____

Confession

In *The Essential Calvin and Hobbes* by Bill Watterson, the cartoon character Calvin says to his tiger friend, Hobbes, "I feel bad that I called Susie names and hurt her feelings. I'm sorry I did it."

"Maybe you should apologize to her," Hobbes suggests.

Calvin ponders this for a moment and replies, "I keep hoping there's a less obvious solution."

When we want to restore our relationship with God, we need to remember that he has a liking for the obvious solution.

—Norm Langston
(Apologies, Restoration)

Dates used:_____

Early in 1993, British police accused two 10-year-old boys of the brutal murder of 2-year-old James Bulger. The two boys pleaded innocence.

During the two-week trial the young defendants responded to police questioning with noticeable inconsistency. The climax of the trial came when the parents of one of the boys assured him that they would always love him. Confronted with irrefutable evidence linking him with the crime and the assurance of his parents' love, the boy confessed in a soft voice, "I killed James."

The miracle of God's love is that he knows how evil we are, yet he loves us. We can confess our worst sins to him, confident that his love will not diminish.

—Greg Asimakoupoulos
(God's Love, Guilt)

Dates used:_____

Conflict

Research indicates that the spotted owls' greatest threat may be not logging, but one of its relatives. For the past fifteen years, the barred owl has migrated westward rapidly. Barred owls, which used to live exclusively east of the Mississippi, compete for the same food as spotted owls but are more aggressive and adaptable.

Sometimes our greatest conflict comes not from outside culture, but from other Christians.

—*Newsweek* (11/25/96)
(Competition, Culture)

Dates used:_____

The *Fort Worth Star-Telegram* reported that firefighters in Genoa, Texas, were accused of deliberately setting more than forty destructive fires. When caught, they stated, "We had nothing to do. We just wanted to get the red lights flashing and the bells clanging."

The job of firefighters is to put out fires, not start them. The job of Christians is to help resolve conflict (Matt. 5:9), not start more of it.

—Gerald Cornelius
(Boredom, Peace)

Dates used:_____

Roberta Croteau wrote in *Aspire:*
In the mid-1980's, singer Amy Grant's life was not as charmed as it appeared. Troubles in her marriage—her husband Gary's cocaine habit and their subsequent talk of divorce—left Amy in one of her darkest moments. She remembers:

"For a few days, I just stayed in bed and mourned my life. The only hope I could see was just junking it all, moving to Europe, and starting everything all over again. It was then my sister, in a last-ditch visit, marched up right beside my bed and said, 'Fine, go to Europe, leave it all behind, start your life again. But before you go, tell (my little girl) how you can sing that Jesus can help her through anything in her life, but that he couldn't help you.' "

The words hit home. Amy and Gary began marriage and personal counseling, slowly rebuilding their relationships with each others and with God.

(Accountability, Divorce)

Dates used:_____

Conscience

Many electronic fire alarms have an internal switch triggered by a beam of light. As long as light is received unbroken by the photo-sensitive receiver, the detector is quiet. But if smoke, moisture, or an insect obstructs the beam for even a split second, the alarm sounds.

Our conscience resembles such an alarm. When sin obstructs our connection with the light of God's Spirit, the conscience signals us that there's life-threatening danger.

—A. D. Sterner
(Holy Spirit, Sin)

Dates used:_____

Contentment

In *Our Daily Bread,* Philip Parham tells the story of a rich industrialist who was disturbed to find a fisherman sitting lazily beside his boat.

"Why aren't you out there fishing?" he asked.

"Because I've caught enough fish for today," said the fisherman.

"Why don't you catch more fish than you need?" the rich man asked.

"What would I do with them?"

"You could earn more money," came the impatient reply, "and buy a better boat so you could go deeper and catch more fish. You could purchase nylon nets, catch even more fish, and make more money. Soon you'd have a fleet of boats and be rich like me."

The fisherman asked, "Then what would I do?"

"You could sit down and enjoy life," said the industrialist.

"What do you think I'm doing now?" the fisherman replied.

—Scott Minnich
(Ambition, Greed)

Dates used:_____

Contentment

The Hope Health Letter (10/95) included this story: Once upon a time, there was a man who lived with his wife, two small children, and his elderly parents in a tiny hut. He tried to be patient and gracious, but the noise and crowded conditions wore him down.

In desperation, he consulted the village wise man. "Do you have a rooster?" asked the wise man.

"Yes," he replied.

"Keep the rooster in the hut with your family, and come see me again next week."

The next week, the man returned and told the wise elder that living conditions were worse than ever, with the rooster crowing and making a mess of the hut.

"Do you have a cow?" asked the wise elder. The man nodded fearfully. "Take your cow into the hut as well, and come see me in a week."

Over the next several weeks, the man—on the advice of the wise elder—made room for a goat, two dogs, and his brother's children.

Finally, he could take no more, and in a fit of anger, kicked out all the animals and guests, leaving only his wife, his children, and his parents. The home suddenly became spacious and quiet, and everyone lived happily ever after.

(Attitude, Family)

Dates used:_____

The comedy film *Cool Runnings* is about the first Jamaican bobsled team to go to the Olympics. John Candy plays a former American gold medalist who becomes a coach to the Jamaican team. The players grow to like the American coach and affectionately dub him "Sled-god."

Later in the story, the coach's dark history comes out. In an Olympics following his gold medal performance, he broke the rules by weighting the U. S. sled, bringing disgrace on himself and his team.

One of the Jamaican bobsledders could not understand why anyone who had already won a gold medal would cheat. Finally he nervously asked the coach to explain.

"I had to win," he said. "I learned something. If you are not happy without a gold medal, you won't be happy with it."

—Randall Bergsma
(Happiness, Motive)

Dates used:_____

Courage

In *A Pretty Good Person*, Lewis Smedes writes:
A federal judge had ordered New Orleans to open its public schools to African-American children, and the white parents decided that if they had to let black children in, they would keep their children out. They let it be known that any black children who came to school would be in for trouble. So the black children stayed home too.

Except Ruby Bridges. Her parents sent her to school all by herself, six years old.

Every morning she walked alone through a heckling crowd to an empty school. White people lined up on both sides of the way and shook their fists at her. They threatened to do terrible things to her if she kept coming to their school. But every morning at ten minutes to eight Ruby walked, head up, eyes ahead, straight through the mob; two U.S. marshals walked ahead of her and two walked behind her. Then she spent the day alone with her teachers inside that big silent school building.

Harvard professor Robert Coles was curious about what went into the making of courageous children like Ruby Bridges. He talked to Ruby's mother and, in his book *The Moral Life of Children*, tells what she said: "There's a lot of people who talk about doing good, and a lot of people who argue about what's good and what's not good," but there are other folks who "just put their lives on the line for what's right."

—Bob Campbell
(Action, Racial Reconciliation)

Dates used:_____

Helen Prejean, the nun whose experiences with death-row inmates led to the movie *Dead Man Walking,* talked recently about creativity:

"In creating, we imitate God. . . . To be a creator is part of what it means to be a human being. I met a guy on death row in Arizona who had nothing. . . . So he would unravel his socks and weave little necklaces with crosses out of the threads. The first time I visited another death-row inmate, he gave me a picture frame he'd made out of gum wrapper foils.

"These men were locked in a small cell 23 out of 24 hours a day; they had absolutely nothing, and still they were reaching out to create something of beauty and worth."

—*Inklings* (Vol. 2, No. 3)
(Beauty, Creation)

Dates used:_____

Criticism

Colonel George Washington Goethals, the man responsible for the completion of the Panama Canal, had big problems with the climate and the geography. But his biggest challenge was the growing criticism back home from those who predicted he'd never finish the project.

Finally, a colleague asked him, "Aren't you going to answer these critics?"

"In time," answered Goethals.

"When?" his partner asked.

"When the canal is finished."

(Accomplishment, Challenges)

Dates used:_____

In the 1993 movie *In the Line of Fire,* Clint Eastwood played Secret Service agent Frank Horrigan. Horrigan had protected the life of the President for more than three decades, but he was haunted by the memory of what had happened thirty years before. Horrigan was a young agent assigned to President Kennedy on that fateful day in Dallas in 1963. When the assassin fired, Horrigan froze in shock.

For thirty years afterward, he wrestled with the ultimate question for a Secret Service agent: Can I take a bullet for the President?

In the climax of the movie, Horrigan did what he had been unable to do earlier: he threw himself into the path of an assassin's bullet to save the chief executive.

Secret Service agents are willing to do such a thing because they believe the President is so valuable to our country and the world that he is worth dying for. Obviously they would not take a bullet for just anyone.

At Calvary the situation was reversed. The President of the Universe actually took a bullet for each of us. At the Cross we see how valuable we are to God.

—Douglas G. Pratt
(Atonement, Substitution)

Dates used:_____

Cross

Tim Miller writes:

My 9-year-old daughter Jennifer was looking forward to our family's vacation. But she became ill, and a long anticipated day at Sea World was replaced by an all-night series of CT scans, x-rays, and blood work at the hospital.

As morning approached, the doctors told my exhausted little girl that she would need to have one more test, a spinal tap. The procedure would be painful, they said. The doctor then asked me if I planned to stay in the room. I nodded, knowing I couldn't leave Jennifer alone during the ordeal.

The doctors gently asked Jennifer to remove all her clothing. She looked at me with childlike modesty as if to ask if that were all right. They had her curl into a tiny ball. I buried my face in hers and hugged her.

When the needle went in, Jennifer cried. As the searing pain increased, she sobbingly repeated, "Daddy, Daddy, Daddy," her voice becoming more earnest with each word. It was as if she were saying, "Oh Daddy, please, can't you do something?"

My tears mingled with hers. My heart was broken. I felt nauseated. Because I loved her, I was allowing her to go through the most agonizing experience of her life, and I could hardly stand it.

In the middle of that spinal tap, my thoughts went to the cross of Christ. What unspeakable pain both the Son and the Father went through—for our sake.

(Empathy, Pain)

Dates used:_____

Bob Russell, senior minister of Southeast Christian Church in Louisville, Kentucky, told this story:

When my father died, there was too much snow at our home in Pennsylvania to have a funeral procession. At the end of the service, the funeral director said, "I'll take your dad's body to the grave." I felt we were leaving something undone, so I gathered five of my relatives, and we piled into a four-wheel-drive vehicle, plowed through ten inches of snow into the cemetery, and got about fifty yards from my dad's grave.

The wind was blowing about twenty-five miles an hour. The six of us lugged that casket down to the grave site. We watched as his body was lowered into that grave.

I wanted to pray before we left. "Lord, this is such a cold, lonely place." I got choked up and battled to keep my composure. Finally I just whispered, "But I thank you that to be absent from the body is to be present in your warm arms. Amen."

—*Preaching Today*
(Heaven, Hope)

Dates used:_____

Death

A boy and his father were driving down a country road on a beautiful spring afternoon, when a bumblebee flew in the car window. The little boy, who was allergic to bee stings, was petrified. The father quickly reached out, grabbed the bee, squeezed it in his hand, and then released it.

The boy grew frantic as it buzzed by him. Once again the father reached out his hand, but this time he pointed to his palm. There stuck in his skin was the stinger of the bee. "Do you see this?" he asked. "You don't need to be afraid anymore. I've taken the sting for you."

We do not need to fear death anymore. Christ has died and risen again. He has taken the sting from death.

—Adrian Uieleman
(Father's Love, Sacrifice)

Dates used:_____

In the movie *Casualties of War,* Michael J. Fox plays Private Erikson, a soldier in Vietnam who is part of a squad that abducts and rapes a young Vietnamese girl. He didn't participate in the crime.

Afterward, as he struggles with what has happened, he says to the other men in his squad, "Just because each of us might at any second be blown away, we're acting like we can do anything we want, as though it doesn't matter what we do. I'm thinking it's just the opposite. Because we might be dead in the next split-second, maybe we gotta be extra careful what we do. Because maybe it matters more. Maybe it matters more than we ever know."

Death, for all of us, is a breath away. And the nearer death is, the closer we are to answering to God for all we have said and done.

—Joel Sarrault
(Conscience, Consequences)

Dates used:_____

Determination

Guideposts (9/95) published the story of Jim Stovall, who became totally blind at age 29. While he still had partial vision, he volunteered at a school for the blind. He was assigned to help a four-year-old boy, blind and severely handicapped. Stovall spent considerable time trying to convince the boy he could tie his own shoes or climb stairs in spite of his limitations.

"No, I can't!" the boy insisted.

"Yes, you can," Stovall replied.

"No, I can't!" The verbal battle went on.

Meanwhile, Stovall fought his own limitations. Because of his deteriorating vision, he decided he had to quit his college courses. On his way to withdraw from college, he decided to resign his volunteer position as well.

"It's just too tough," he explained. "I can't do it."

"Yes, you can!" said a little voice beside him. It was the four-year-old who refused to tie his shoes.

"No, I can't!" said Stovall with conviction.

"Yes, you can!"

Stovall realized if he didn't continue, the child would give up too. So Stovall stayed in school and graduated three-and-a-half years later. The same week he graduated, his little friend tied his shoes *and* climbed a flight of stairs.

Philippians tell us we "can do all things through Christ who gives us strength."

—David Chotka
(Example, Perseverance)

Dates used:_____

From time to time, lobsters have to leave their shells in order to grow. They need the shell to protect them from being torn apart, yet when they grow, the old shell must be abandoned. If they did not abandon it, the old shell would soon become their prison—and finally their casket.

The tricky part for the lobster is the brief period of time between when the old shell is discarded and the new one is formed. During that terribly vulnerable period, the transition must be scary to the lobster. Currents gleefully cartwheel them from coral to kelp. Hungry schools of fish are ready to make them a part of their food chain. For awhile at least, that old shell must look pretty good.

We are not so different from lobsters. To change and grow, we must sometimes shed our shells— a structure, a framework—we've depended on. Discipleship means being so committed to Christ that when he bids us to follow, we will change, risk, grow, and leave our "shells" behind.

—Brent Mitchell
(Growth, Transitions)

Dates used:_____

Distractions

In one scene of the popular movie *Robin Hood, The Prince of Thieves,* Kevin Costner as Robin comes to a young man taking aim at an archery target. Robin asks, "Can you shoot amid distractions?"

Just before the boy releases the string, Robin pokes his ear with the feathers of an arrow. The boy's shot flies high by several feet.

After the laughter of those watching dies down, Maid Marian, standing behind the boy, asks Robin, "Can you?"

Robin Hood raises his bow and takes aim. Just as he releases the arrow, Maid Marian leans beside him and flirtatiously blows into his face. The arrow misses the target, glances off the tree behind it, and scarcely misses a bystander.

Distractions come in all types, and whether they are painful or pleasant, the result is the same: we miss God's mark.

—Penney F. Nichols
(Sin, Temptation)

Dates used:_____

M r. Alter's fifth-grade class at Lake Elementary School in Oceanside, California, included fourteen boys who had no hair. Only one, however, had no choice in the matter.

In an Associated Press story (March 1994), Ian O'Gorman, undergoing chemotherapy for lymphoma, faced the prospect of having his hair fall out in clumps. So he had his head shaved. But then thirteen of his classmates shaved their heads, so Ian wouldn't feel out of place.

Ten-year-old Kyle Hanslik started it all. He talked to some other boys, and before long they all trekked to the barber shop. "The last thing he would want is to not fit in," said Kyle. "We just wanted to make him feel better."

"Carry each other's burdens, and in this way you will fulfill the law of Christ" (Gal. 6:2).

—Sherman L. Burford
(Caring, Compassion)

Dates used:_____

Encouragement

For years William Wilberforce pushed Britain's Parliament to abolish slavery. Discouraged, he was about to give up. His elderly friend, John Wesley, heard of it and from his deathbed called for pen and paper.

With trembling hand, Wesley wrote: "Unless God has raised you up for this very thing, you will be worn out by the opposition of men and devils. But if God be for you, who can be against you? Are all of them stronger than God?

"Oh be not weary of well-doing! Go on, in the name of God and in the power of his might, till even American slavery shall vanish away before it."

Wesley died six days later. But Wilberforce fought for forty-five more years and in 1833, three days before his own death, saw slavery abolished in Britain.

Even the greatest ones need encouragement.

—Carol Porter
(Opposition, Perseverance)

Dates used:_____

Portable camcorders have a battery pack for
power. Instructions typically recommend that
users allow the battery pack to completely discharge
before recharging, especially the first few times. This
actually increases the endurance of the battery.

In like manner, our trials "discharge" us, emptying
us of our dependence on human strength and
increasing our capacity to receive God's limitless
power.

—Philip Bourdon
(Dependence, God's Power)

Dates used:_____

N early half (48 percent) of American workers admitted to taking unethical or illegal actions in the past year. *USA Today* (4/4/97) revealed the top five types of unethical/illegal behavior that workers say they have engaged in over the past year because of pressure:

- Cut corners on quality control
- Covered up incidents
- Abused or lied about sick days
- Lied to or deceived customers
- Put inappropriate pressure on others.

—survey by Ethics Officers Association and the
American Society of Chartered Life Underwriters
and Chartered Financial Consultants

(Dishonesty, Lying)

Dates used:_____

The Oakland, California, police force recently unveiled its first "lowrider" police car. The vehicle has the standard logo, lights, and siren, but also includes chrome wheels, hydraulic lifts, and a 500-watt sound system. The car was put on the force to help officers build better relationships with inner-city kids.

Paul applied the same principle to evangelism in 1 Corinthians 9:22–23: "I have become all things to all men so that by all possible means I might save some."

—Chip Johnston
(Relationships, Strategy)

Dates used:_____

Evangelism

Louis Pasteur, the pioneer of immunology, lived at a time when thousands of people died each year of rabies. Pasteur had worked for years on a vaccine. Just as he was about to begin experimenting on himself, a nine-year-old, Joseph Meister, was bitten by a rabid dog. The boy's mother begged Pasteur to experiment on her son. Pasteur injected Joseph for ten days—and the boy lived.

Decades later, of all the things Pasteur could have had etched on his headstone, he asked for three words: JOSEPH MEISTER LIVED.

Our greatest legacy will be those who live eternally because of our efforts.

—R. Wayne Willis
(Legacy, Service)

Dates used:_____

I n *Conspiracy of Kindness,* Steve Sjogren (pro-
nounced Show-gren) tells the true story of Joe
Delaney and his eight-year-old son, Jared, who were
playing catch in their backyard.

Jared asked, "Dad, is there a God?"

Joe replied that he went to church only a few
times when he was a kid; he really had no idea.

Jared ran into the house. "I'll be right back!" he
yelled.

Moments later he returned with a helium balloon
from the circus, a pen, and an index card. "I'm going
to send God an airmail message," Jared explained.
"Dear God," wrote Jared, "if you are real, and you are
there, send people who know you to Dad and me."

God, I hope you're watching, Joe thought, as they
watched the balloon and message sail away.

Two days later, Joe and Jared pulled into a car
wash sponsored by Sjogren's church. When Joe
asked, "How much?" Sjogren answered, "It's free. No
strings attached. We just want to show God's love in
a practical way."

"Are you guys Christians, the kind of Christians
who believe in God?" Joe asked.

Sjogren said, "Yes, we're *that* kind of Christians."

From that encounter, Steve led Joe to faith in Christ.

Many people may be only one act of kindness
from meeting a true Christian.

—Tom Lundeen
(Kindness, Ministry)

Dates used:_____

Evangelism

Doug Nichols shares this story:

While serving with Operation Mobilization in India in 1967, tuberculosis forced me into a sanitarium for several months. I sensed many weren't happy about a rich American (to them all Americans were rich) being in a free, government-run sanitarium. I did not yet speak the language, but I tried to give Christian literature written in their language to the patients, doctors, and nurses. Everyone politely refused.

The first few nights I woke around 2 A.M., coughing. One morning during my coughing spell, I noticed one of the older and sicker patients across the aisle trying to get out of bed. He would sit up on the edge of the bed and try to stand, but in weakness would fall back into bed. I didn't understand what he was trying to do. He finally fell back into bed exhausted. I heard him crying softly.

The next morning I realized he had been trying to get up and walk to the bathroom! The stench in our ward was awful. Other patients yelled insults at the man. Angry nurses moved him roughly from side to side as they cleaned up the mess. One nurse even slapped him. The old man curled into a ball and wept.

The next night I again woke up coughing. I noticed the man across the aisle again try to stand. Like the night before, he fell back whimpering. I don't like bad smells, and I didn't want to become involved, but I got out of bed and went over to him. When I touched his shoulder, his eyes opened wide with fear. I smiled, put my arms under him, and picked him up.

He was very light due to old age and advanced TB. I carried him to the washroom, which was just a filthy, small room with a hole in the floor. I stood behind him with my arms under his armpits as he took care of himself. After he finished, I picked him up, and carried him back to his bed. As I laid him down, he kissed me on the cheek, smiled, and said something I couldn't understand.

The next morning another patient woke me and handed me a steaming cup of tea. He motioned with his hands that he wanted a tract.

As the sun rose, other patients approached and indicated they also wanted the booklets I had tried to distribute before. Throughout the day nurses, interns, and doctors asked for literature.

Weeks later an evangelist who spoke the language visited me, and discovered that several had put their trust in Christ as Savior as a result of reading the literature.

What did it take to reach these people with the gospel? It wasn't health, the ability to speak their language, or a persuasive talk. I simply took a trip to the bathroom.

(Compassion, Ministry)

Dates used:_____

Evangelism

In 1992, a Los Angeles County parking control officer came upon a brown El Dorado Cadillac illegally parked next to the curb on street-sweeping day.

The officer dutifully wrote out a ticket. Ignoring the man seated at the driver's wheel, the officer reached inside the open car window and placed the $30 citation on the dashboard.

The driver of the car made no excuses. No argument ensued—and with good reason. The driver of the car had been shot in the head ten to twelve hours before but was sitting up, stiff as a board, slumped slightly forward, with blood on his face. He was dead.

The officer, preoccupied with ticket-writing, was unaware of anything out of the ordinary. He got back in his car and drove away.

Many people around us are "dead in transgressions and sins." What should catch our attention most is their need, not their offenses. They don't need a citation; they need a Savior.

—Greg Asimakoupoulos
(Attention, Neglect)

Dates used:_____

Andrew Meekens, an elder in the International Evangelical Church of Addis Ababa, was one of those who died on November 23, 1996, when a hijacked jet ran out of fuel and crashed near the Comoros Islands.

According to survivors of the crash, after the pilot announced he would attempt an emergency landing, Meekens stood up and spoke, calming passengers on the Ethiopian Airlines flight. Meekens then presented the gospel of Jesus Christ, and invited people to respond.

A surviving flight attendant said that about twenty people accepted salvation, including a flight attendant who did not survive the crash.

We preach as dying people to dying people.

—*Beacon* (1/97)
(Courage, Salvation)

Dates used:_____

Evangelism

On his night job at Taco Bell, 17-year-old Nicholas Zenns was taking orders at the drive-up window. He heard a woman scream, turned, and saw a very pregnant Devorah Anderson standing in front of him. The high-school student pulled off his headset, called the paramedics, and tried to make the woman comfortable. But the baby wouldn't wait. "The baby's head just popped out into my hands," Nicholas said.

Paramedics finally arrived and took baby and parents to the hospital. Nicholas cleaned up, "sterilized my hands about a thousand times," and finished his shift.

Nicholas says this event changed his perspective. "Things have been pretty bad in my life lately, and then I got to do this. I'm really glad."

In the same way, nothing makes life more meaningful than leading someone to new birth in Christ.

—*San Diego Union-Tribune* (5/23/96)
(Outreach, Salvation)

Dates used:_____

According to the *Bergen* (N.J.) *Record,* the zoo in Copenhagen, Denmark, recently put a human couple on display. Henrik Lehmann and Malene Botoft live in a see-through cage, in the primate display, next to the baboons and the monkeys.

Their 320-square-foot habitat has a living room with furniture, a computer, a television, and stereo. The kitchen and bedroom are part of the display. Only the bathroom is excluded from public view.

Unlike their neighbors, who aren't allowed out, the two humans occasionally leave their fishbowl existence to shop and water the flowers on their porch back home.

"We don't notice visitors anymore," said Lehmann. "If I want to pick my nose or my toes now, I do it."

We would do well to remember that people are watching the way we live. "In everything set them an example by doing what is good" (Titus 2:7).

—*Parade Magazine* (12/29/96)
(Marriage, Privacy)

Dates used:_____

Example | 57

Expectations

A traveler nearing a great city asked an old man seated by the road, "What are the people like in this city?"

The man replied, "What were they like where you came from?"

"A terrible lot," the traveler reported. "Mean, untrustworthy, detestable in all respects."

"Ah," said the old man. "You will find them the same in the city ahead."

Scarcely had the first traveler gone on his way when another stopped to inquire about the people in the city before him. Again the old man asked about the people in the place the traveler had just left.

"They were fine people, honest, industrious, and generous to a fault. I was sorry to leave," declared the second traveler.

Responded the wise one, "So you will find them in the city ahead."

—Boyd Seevers
(Attitude, Relationships)

Dates used:_____

"First day in the sixth grade, I'll never forget it," recalls Jesse Jackson, who ran for president of the United States in 1988. "My teacher was Miz Shelton, and she began writing these long words on the blackboard we couldn't understand, never even heard of before. We all looked around and started whispering to each other, 'She got the wrong class. She thinks we the eighth-grade class.'

"Somebody finally called out, 'Uh, Miz Shelton? Those are eighth-grade words. We only the sixth grade here.'

"She turned around. 'I know what grade you are. I work here. And you'll learn every one of these words, and a lot more like them, before this year is over. I will not teach down to you. One of you little brats just might be mayor or governor, or even President, some day, and I'm gonna make sure you'll be ready.'

"And she turned back and went right on writing." At that time, Jackson says, her proposition prompted no glow of possibility in him. "Aim to be governor? Even aim to be mayor, when in Greenville then there wasn't a single African-American on the Board of Education, in the police department, the fire department? And aim to be President?!"

Before any great accomplishment, someone must have a vision.

—*The New Yorker* (2/10/92)
(Hope, Vision)

Dates used:_____

Failure

Dani Tyler, third-base star for the U.S. women's Olympic softball team, hit a home run. Or so she thought. In her excitement rounding the bases, she accidentally stepped over home plate. The umpire disallowed the run. Because of that one misstep, the U.S. team lost in extra innings 2–1, only their second international loss in ten years.

The next evening, Tyler played well. *Sports Illustrated* writer Peter King (8/12/96) asked her why the mistake hadn't become a mental ball-and-chain.

"Well, I didn't want to get out of bed this morning," she admitted. "But this is sports. One play doesn't make a game, and one play won't define my life. I've never been the best athlete, but I try to have the best attitude and work the hardest. What happened was a freak thing. It's over. If I whine about it, or make excuses, or argue, what happens? I look like a jerk."

(Adversity, Excuses)

Dates used:_____

William Plummer and Bonnie Bell wrote in *People* magazine:

The Northwestern University Wildcats shocked the world of college football in 1995 by making it to the Rose Bowl Tournament. The man behind the team's turnaround was coach Gary Barnett. . . . [Barnett] was determined to prove that kids at the Big Ten's smallest and most academically demanding school could play football. He ordered a Tournament of Roses flag for the football building and kept a silk rose on his desk to remind everyone where they were headed.

"At the first meeting," says kicker Sam Valenzisi, "he told us we needed belief without evidence. He asked, 'Do you know what that is? That's faith.' "

—Sherman L. Burford
(Achievement, Belief)

Dates used:_____

Faith

B en Patterson, in *Waiting,* writes:
In 1988, three friends and I climbed Mount
Lyell, the highest peak in Yosemite National Park.
Our base camp was less than 2,000 feet from the
peak, but the climb to the top and back was to take
the better part of a day, due in large part to the difficulty of the glacier we had to cross to get to the top.
The morning of the climb we started out chattering
and cracking jokes.

As the hours passed, the two more experienced
mountaineers opened up a wide gap between me and
my less-experienced companion. Being competitive
by nature, I began to look for shortcuts to beat them
to the top. I thought I saw one to the right of an
outcropping of rock—so I went, deaf to the protests
of my companion.

Perhaps it was the effect of the high altitude, but
the significance of the two experienced climbers not
choosing this path did not register in my consciousness. It should have, for thirty minutes later I was
trapped in a cul-de-sac of rock atop the Lyell Glacier,
looking down several hundred feet of a sheer slope of
ice, pitched at about a forty-five degree angle.... I was
only about ten feet from the safety of a rock, but one
little slip and I wouldn't stop sliding until I landed in
the valley floor some fifty miles away! It was nearly
noon, and the warm sun had the glacier glistening
with slippery ice. I was stuck, and I was scared.

It took an hour for my experienced climbing
friends to find me. Standing on the rock I wanted to
reach, one of them leaned out and used an ice ax to

chip two little footsteps in the glacier. Then he gave me the following instructions: "Ben, you must step out from where you are and put your foot where the first foothold is. When your foot touches it, without a moment's hesitation swing your other foot across and land it on the next step. When you do that, reach out and I will take your hand and pull you to safety."

That sounded real good to me. It was the next thing he said that made me more frightened than ever. "But listen carefully: As you step across, do not lean into the mountain! If anything, lean out a bit. Otherwise, your feet may fly out from under you, and you will start sliding down."

I don't like precipices. When I am on the edge of a cliff, my instincts are to lie down and hug the mountain, to become one with it, not to lean away from it! But that was what my good friend was telling me to do. For a moment, based solely on what I believed to be the good will and good sense of my friend, I decided to say no to what I felt, to stifle my impulse to cling to the security of the mountain, to lean out, step out, and traverse the ice to safety. It took less than two seconds to find out if my faith was well founded.

To save us, God often tells us to do things that are the opposite of our natural inclination. Is God loving and faithful? Can we trust him?

He is. We can.

(Obedience, Trust)

Dates used:_____

Faith

The mighty Niagara River plummets some 180 feet at the American and Horseshoe Falls. Before the falls, there are violent, turbulent rapids. Farther upstream, however, where the river's current flows more gently, boats are able to navigate. Just before the Welland River empties into the Niagara, a pedestrian walkway spans the river. Posted on this bridge's pylons is a warning sign for all boaters: DO YOU HAVE AN ANCHOR? followed by, DO YOU KNOW HOW TO USE IT?

Faith, like an anchor, is something we need to have and use to avoid spiritual cataclysm.

—Paul Adams
(Crisis, Preparation)

Dates used:_____

While Eric Hulstrand of Binford, North Dakota, was preaching one Sunday, an elderly woman, Mary, fainted and struck her head on the end of the pew. Immediately, an EMT in the congregation called an ambulance.

As they strapped her to a stretcher and got ready to head out the door, Mary regained consciousness. She motioned for her daughter to come near. Everyone thought she was summoning her strength to convey what could be her final words. The daughter leaned over until her ear was at her mother's mouth.

"My offering is in my purse," she whispered.

(Generosity, Stewardship)

Dates used:_____

Faithfulness

Newsweek (11/19/90) ran an article titled "Letters in the Sand," a compilation of letters written by military personnel to family and friends in the States during the Gulf War.

One was written by Marine Corporal Preston Coffer. He told a friend, "We are talking about Marines, not the Boy Scouts. We all joined the service knowing full well what might be expected of us." He signed off with the Marine motto, *Semper Fi*, Latin for "always faithful."

The Bible says, "Now it is required that those who have been given a trust must prove faithful" (1 Cor. 4:2).

—Richie Lewis
(Dedication, Expectations)

Dates used:_____

When she turned 21, Tammy Harris from Roanoke, Virginia, began searching for her biological mother. After a year, she had not succeeded. What she didn't know was that her mother, Joyce Schultz, had been trying to locate her for twenty years.

According to a recent Associated Press story, there was one more thing Tammy didn't know: Her mother was one of her coworkers at the convenience store where she worked! One day Joyce overheard Tammy talking with another coworker about trying to find her mother. Soon they were comparing birth certificates.

When Tammy realized that the co-worker she had known was, in fact, her mother, she fell into her arms. "We held on for the longest time," Tammy said. "It was the best day of my life."

Each week we rub shoulders with people whom we may barely notice. But if they share a birth in Christ, they are our dearest relatives. How precious is the family of God!

—B. Paul Greene
(Church, Relationships)

Dates used:_____

Fatherhood

At a 1994 Promise Keepers' conference in Denton, Texas, pastor James Ryle told his story:

When he was 2 years old, his father was sent to prison. When he was 7, authorities placed him in an orphanage. At 19, he had a car wreck that killed a friend. He sold drugs to raise money for his legal fee, and the law caught up to him. He was arrested, charged with a felony, and sent to prison.

While in prison James accepted Christ, and after he served his time, he eventually went into the ministry. Years later he sought out his father to reconcile with him. When they got together, the conversation turned to prison life.

James's father asked, "Which prison were you in?"

James told him, and his father was taken aback. "I helped build that prison," he said. He had been a welder who went from place to place building penitentiaries.

Pastor Ryle concluded, "I was in the prison my father built."

A father's example builds a place to live for his children. Will it be a house, or a prison?

—Larry Pillow
(Example, Legacy)

Dates used:_____

G reg Norman intimidates most other professional golfers with his ice-cold stoicism. He learned his hard-nosed tactics from his father. "I used to see my father, getting off a plane or something, and I'd want to hug him," he recalled once. "But he'd only shake my hand." Commenting on his aloofness going into the 1996 Masters golf tournament, Norman said, "Nobody really knows me out here."

After leading golf's most prestigious event from the start, Norman blew a six-shot lead in the last round, losing to rival Nick Faldo.

Rick Reilly writes, "Now, as Faldo made one last thrust into Norman's heart with a fifteen-foot birdie putt on the seventy-second hole, the two of them came toward each other, Norman trying to smile, looking for a handshake and finding himself in the warmest embrace instead.

"As they held that hug, held it even as both of them cried, Norman changed just a little. 'I wasn't crying because I'd lost,' Norman said the next day. 'I've lost a lot of golf tournaments before. I'll lose a lot more. I cried because I'd never felt that from another man before. I've never had a hug like that in my life.' "

—*Sports Illustrated* (12/30/96)
(Brotherhood, Men)

Dates used:_____

Final Judgment

S teve Winger from Lubbock, Texas, writes about his last college test—a final in a logic class known for its difficult exams:

To help us on our test, the professor told us we could bring as much information to the exam as we could fit on a piece of notebook paper. Most students crammed as many facts as possible on their 8-1/2 x 11 inch sheet of paper.

But one student walked into class, put a piece of notebook paper on the floor, and had an advanced logic student stand on the paper. The advanced logic student told him everything he needed to know. He was the only student to receive an A.

The ultimate final exam will come when we stand before God and he asks, "Why should I let you in?" On our own we cannot pass that exam. But we have Someone who will stand in for us.

(Intercession, Reconciliation)

Dates used:_____

Finishing Well

A t 7 P.M. on October 20, 1968, a few thousand spectators remained in the Mexico City Olympic Stadium. It was cool and dark. The last of the marathon runners, each exhausted, were being carried off to first-aid stations. More than an hour earlier, Mamo Wolde of Ethiopia—looking as fresh as when he started the race—crossed the finish line, the winner of the 26-mile, 385-yard event.

As the remaining spectators prepared to leave, those sitting near the marathon gates suddenly heard the sound of sirens and police whistles. All eyes turned to the gate. A lone figure wearing number 36 and the colors of Tanzania entered the stadium. His name was John Stephen Akhwari. He was the last man to finish the marathon. He had fallen during the race and injured his knee and ankle. Now, with his leg bloodied and bandaged, he grimaced with each hobbling step around the 400-meter track.

The spectators rose and applauded him. After crossing the finish line, Akhwari slowly walked off the field. Later, a reporter asked Akhwari the question on everyone's mind: "Why did you continue the race after you were so badly injured?"

He replied, "My country did not send me 7,000 miles to start the race. They sent me 7,000 miles to finish it."

"Let us run with perseverance the race marked out for us" (Heb. 12:1).

—Wes Thompson
(Perseverance, Tenacity)

Dates used:_____

Finishing Well

In a recent NCAA cross-country championship held in Riverside, California, 123 of the 128 runners missed a turn. One competitor, Mike Delcavo, stayed on the 10,000-meter course and began waving for fellow runners to follow him. Delcavo was able to convince only four other runners to go with him.

Asked what his competitors thought of his mid-race decision not to follow the crowd, Delcavo responded, "They thought it was funny that I went the right way."

Delcavo ran correctly. In the same way, our goal is to run correctly—to finish the race marked out for us by Christ. We can rejoice over those who have courage to follow, ignoring the laughter of the crowd.

"I have fought the good fight, I have finished the race, I have kept the faith. Now there is in store for me the crown of righteousness" (2 Tim. 4:7–8).

—Loren D. McBain
(Courage, Obedience)

Dates used:_____

On Day Six of the ill-fated mission of Apollo 13, the astronauts needed to make a critical course correction. If they failed, they might never return to Earth.

To conserve power, they shut down the onboard computer that steered the craft. Yet the astronauts needed to conduct a thirty-nine-second burn of the main engines. How to steer?

Astronaut Jim Lovell determined that if they could keep a fixed point in space in view through their tiny window, they could steer the craft manually. That focal point turned out to be their destination—Earth.

As shown in 1995's hit movie, *Apollo 13,* for thirty-nine agonizing seconds, Lovell focused on keeping the earth in view. By not losing sight of that reference point, the three astronauts avoided disaster.

Scripture reminds us that to finish your life mission successfully, "Fix your eyes on Jesus, the author and perfecter of our faith" (Heb. 12:2).

—Stephen Nordbye
(Completion, Success)

Dates used:_____

Focus

Warren Bennis, in *Why Leaders Can't Lead,* writes:

The flying Wallendas are perhaps the world's greatest family of aerialists and tightrope walkers. . . . I was struck with [Karl Wallenda's] capacity for concentration on the intention, the task, the decision. I was even more intrigued when, several months later, Wallenda fell to his death while walking a tightrope without a safety net between two high-rise buildings in San Juan, Puerto Rico. . . .

Later, Wallenda's wife said that before her husband had fallen, for the first time since she had known him, he had been concentrating on falling, instead of on walking the tightrope. He had personally supervised the attachment of the guide wires, which he had never done before.

Often the difference between success and failure, life and death, is the direction we're looking.

—Rex Bonar
(Failure, Success)

Dates used:_____

Tom Friends of *The New York Times* asked coach Jimmy Johnson what he told his players before leading the Dallas Cowboys onto the field for the 1993 Super Bowl.

"I told them that if I laid a two-by-four across the floor, everybody there would walk across it and not fall, because our focus would be on walking the length of that board. But if I put that same board 10 stories high between two buildings, only a few would make it, because the focus would be on falling."

Johnson told his players not to focus on the crowd, the media, or the possibility of falling, but to focus on each play of the game as if it were a good practice session. The Cowboys won the game 52–7.

A Christian must not focus on what people think, but only on what is "excellent or praiseworthy" (Phil. 4:8).

—Steve Chandler
100 Ways to Motivate Yourself
(Target, Thoughts)

Dates used:_____

Forgiveness

The picture haunted him. Like many Americans, Rev. John Plummer, minister of Bethany United Methodist church in Purcellville, Virginia, was moved by the Vietnam-era Pulitzer-Prize-winning photo of 9-year-old Phan Thi Kim Phuc, naked and horribly burned, running from a napalm attack.

But for Plummer, that picture had special significance. In 1972 he was responsible for setting up the air strike on the village of Trang Bang—a strike approved after he was twice assured there were no civilians in the area.

Plummer said that even though he knew he had done everything possible to make sure the area was clear of civilians, he experienced new pain each time he saw the picture. He wanted to tell Kim Phuc how sorry he was.

After becoming a Christian in 1990, Plummer felt called to the ministry and attended seminary. In June 1996 he learned that Kim Phuc was still alive and living in Toronto. The next month he attended a military reunion and met someone who knew both Kim Phuc and the photographer. Plummer learned that on that fateful day in 1972, Kim Phuc and her family were hiding in a pagoda in Trang Bang when a bomb hit the building. Kim Phuc and others ran into the street, where they were hit by napalm being dropped from another plane. She tore off her burning clothing as she fled. Two of her cousins were killed.

The photographer and other journalists poured water from canteens on her burns. She collapsed moments after the famous photo and was rushed by car to a hospital. The girl spent fourteen months in hospitals and was operated on by a San Francisco plastic surgeon.

Plummer learned that Kim Phuc was speaking at the Vietnam Veterans Memorial in Washington, D. C. He went and heard Kim Phuc say that if she ever met the pilot of the plane, she would tell him she forgives him and that they cannot change the past, but she hoped they could work together in the future.

Plummer was able to get word to Kim Phuc that the man she wanted to meet was there.

"She saw my grief, my pain, my sorrow," Plummer wrote in an article in the *Virginia Advocate*. "She held out her arms to me and embraced me. All I could say was, 'I'm sorry; I'm so sorry; I'm sorry' over and over again. At the same time she was saying, 'It's all right; it's all right; I forgive; I forgive.' "

Plummer learned that although she was raised a Buddhist, Kim Phuc became a Christian in 1982.

—Evangelical Press News Service
(Pardon, Restitution)

Dates used:_____

Forgiveness

The story of "Wrong Way Riegels" is a familiar one, but it bears repeating.

On New Year's Day, 1929, Georgia Tech played UCLA in the Rose Bowl. In that game a young man named Roy Riegels recovered a fumble for UCLA. Picking up the loose ball, he lost his direction and ran sixty-five yards toward the wrong goal line. One of his teammates, Benny Lom, ran him down and tackled him just before he scored for the opposing team. Several plays later, the Bruins had to punt. Tech blocked the kick and scored a safety, demoralizing the UCLA team.

The strange play came in the first half. At halftime the UCLA players filed off the field and into the dressing room. As others sat down on the benches and the floor, Riegels sat down in a corner, and put his face in his hands.

A football coach usually has a great deal to say to his team during halftime. That day Coach Price was quiet. No doubt he was trying to decide what to do with Riegels.

When the timekeeper came in and announced that there were three minutes before playing time, Coach Price looked at the team and said, "Men, the same team that played the first half will start the second." The players got up and started out, all but Riegels. He didn't budge. The coach looked back and called to him. Riegels didn't move. Coach Price went over to where Riegels sat and said, "Roy, didn't you hear me? The same team that played the first half will start the second."

Roy Riegels looked up, his cheeks wet with tears. "Coach," he said, "I can't do it. I've ruined you. I've ruined the university's reputation. I've ruined myself. I can't face that crowd out there."

Coach Price reached out, put his hand on Riegels's shoulder, and said, "Roy, get up and go on back. The game is only half over."

Riegels finally did get up. He went onto the field, and the fans saw him play hard and play well.

All of us have run a long way in the wrong direction. Because of God's mercy, however, the game is only half over.

—Wayne Rouse
(Mistakes, Starting Over)

Dates used:_____

Forgiveness

Ronald Reagan's attitude after the 1982 attempt on his life made an impression on his daughter, Patti Davis:

"The following day my father said he knew his physical healing was directly dependent on his ability to forgive John Hinckley. By showing me that forgiveness is the key to everything, including physical health and healing, he gave me an example of Christ-like thinking."

—*Angels Don't Die*
(Example, Healing)

Dates used:_____

Freedom does not mean the absence of constraints or moral absolutes. Suppose a skydiver at 10,000 feet announces to the rest of the group, "I'm not using a parachute this time. I want freedom!"

The fact is that a skydiver is constrained by a greater law—the law of gravity. But when the skydiver chooses the "constraint" of the parachute, she is free to enjoy the exhilaration.

God's moral laws act the same way: they restrain, but they are absolutely necessary to enjoy the exhilaration of real freedom.

—Colin Campbell
(Law, Obedience)

Dates used:_____

Freedom

Eating lunch at a small cafe, Mark Reed of Camarillo, California, saw a sparrow hop through the open door and peck at the crumbs near his table. When the crumbs were gone, the sparrow hopped to the window ledge, spread its wings, and took flight. Brief flight. It crashed against the window pane and fell to the floor.

The bird quickly recovered and tried again. Crash. And again. Crash.

Mark got up and attempted to shoo the sparrow out the door, but the closer he got, the harder it threw itself against the pane. He nudged it with his hand. That sent the sparrow fluttering along the ledge, hammering its beak at the glass.

Finally, Mark reached out and gently caught the bird, folding his fingers around its wings and body. It weighed almost nothing. He thought of how powerless and vulnerable the sparrow must have felt. At the door he released it, and the sparrow sailed away.

As Mark did with the sparrow, God takes us captive only to set us free.

(Captive, God's Love)

Dates used:_____

When you stand beside a 747 jet on the runway, its massive weight and size makes it seem incapable of breaking the holds of gravity.

But when the power of its engines combines with the laws of aerodynamics, the plane is able to lift itself to 35,000 feet and travel at 600 miles per hour. Gravity is still pulling on the plane, but as long as it obeys the laws of aerodynamics, it can break free from the bonds of earth.

"Through Christ Jesus the law of the Spirit of life set me free from the law of sin and death" (Rom. 8:2).

—Bill Morris
(Law, Obedience)

Dates used:_____

Future

In an essay entitled "Good Guys Finish First
(Sometimes)," Andrew Bagnato told the following
story:

Following a rags-to-riches season that led them to
the Rose Bowl—their first in decades—Northwestern
University's Wildcats met with coach Gary Barnett
for the opening of spring training.

As players found their seats, Barnett announced
that he was going to hand out the awards that many
Wildcats had earned in 1995. Some players
exchanged glances. Barnett does not normally dwell
on the past. But as the coach continued to call players forward and handed them placards proclaiming
their achievements, they were cheered on by their
teammates.

One of the other coaches gave Barnett a placard
representing his seventeen national coach-of-the-year
awards. Then, as the applause subsided, Barnett
walked to a trash can marked "1995." He took an
admiring glance at his placard, then dumped it in the
can.

In the silence that followed, one by one, the team's
stars dumped their placards on top of Barnett's.
Barnett had shouted a message without uttering a
word: "What you did in 1995 was terrific, lads. But
look at the calendar: It's 1996."

*It's great to celebrate the accomplishments of the
past. But with God, our best days are always ahead.*

—*Chicago Tribune Magazine* (9/1/96)
(Achievement, Nostalgia)

Dates used:_____

A nne Keegan's article "Blue Christmas" was a collection of Christmas stories told by Chicago police officers. One was the story of George White.

George lived in a rented room at the YMCA. He had one set of clothes, shoes wrapped with rubber bands to keep the soles from flopping, and a threadbare black overcoat. He spent his mornings napping in an old metal chair by the heater in the back of the 18th District office.

Two officers, Kitowski and Mitch, took an interest in the old man, occasionally slipping him a few bucks. They found out that Billy the Greek over at the G&W grill gave him a hot breakfast every morning, no charge.

The two policemen and their families decided to have George as their guest for Christmas dinner. They gave him presents, which he unwrapped carefully.

As they drove him back to the Y, George asked, "Are these presents really mine to keep?" They assured him they were. "Then we must stop at the G&W before I go home," he said. With that, George began rewrapping his presents.

When they walked into the restaurant, Billy the Greek was there as always. "You been good to me, Billy," said George. "Now I can be good to you. Merry Christmas." George gave all his presents away on the spot.

Generosity is natural when a grateful attitude prevails.

—*Chicago Tribune Magazine* (12/24/95)

(Attitude, Selflessness)

Dates used:_____

Gentleness

U nder the headline "Gear Blamed in Crash That
Killed Senator," the April 29, 1992, issue of the
Chicago Tribune reported:

A stripped gear in the propeller controls of a com-
muter plane caused it to nosedive into the Georgia
woods last April, killing former U.S. Senator John
Tower of Texas and twenty-two others, the government concluded Tuesday.

A gear that adjusted the pitch of the left engine's
propellers was slowly worn away by an opposing
part with a harder titanium coating, the National
Transportation Safety Board said.

"It acted like a file, and over time it wore down the
teeth that controlled the propeller," said acting board
chairman Susan Coughlin.

*Like the titanium-coated gear that wore away the
softer gear engaged to it, so one abrasive, unkind
spouse or friend can wear away the spirit of another.*

(Relationships, Unkindness)

Dates used:_____

Fortune magazine reported that the nation's top twenty-five philanthropists gave away more than $1.5 billion in 1996. The most generous was George Soros, president of Soros Fund Management, who donated $350 million last year.

Of the top twenty-five philanthropists, only four inherited fortunes. Most attributed their generosity in part to religious backgrounds. And most were donors even before they became wealthy.

(Generosity, Stewardship)

Dates used:_____

Giving

In *Run with the Horses,* Eugene Peterson writes about seeing a family of birds teaching the young to fly. Three young swallows were perched on a dead branch that stretched out over a lake.

"One adult swallow got alongside the chicks and started shoving them out toward the end of the branch—pushing, pushing, pushing. The end one fell off. Somewhere between the branch and the water four feet below, the wings started working, and the fledgling was off on his own. Then the second one.

"The third was not to be bullied. At the last possible moment his grip on the branch loosened just enough so that he swung downward, then tightened again, bulldog tenacious. The parent was without sentiment. He pecked at the desperately clinging talons until it was more painful for the poor chick to hang on than risk the insecurities of flying. The grip was released, and the inexperienced wings began pumping. The mature swallow knew what the chick did not—that it would fly—that there was no danger in making it do what it was perfectly designed to do.

"Birds have feet and can walk. Birds have talons and can grasp a branch securely. They can walk; they can cling. But flying is their characteristic action, and not until they fly are they living at their best, gracefully and beautifully.

"Giving is what we do best. It is the air into which we were born. It is the action that was designed into us before our birth. . . . Some of us try desperately to hold on to ourselves, to live for ourselves. We look so bedraggled and pathetic doing it, hanging on to the dead branch of a bank account for dear life, afraid to risk ourselves on the untried wings of giving. We don't think we can live generously because we have never tried. But the sooner we start, the better, for we are going to have to give up our lives finally, and the longer we wait, the less time we have for the soaring and swooping life of grace."

—David B. Jackson
(Adversity, Miserliness)

Dates used:_____

God's Glory

During construction of Emerson Hall at Harvard University, president Charles Eliot invited psychologist and philosopher William James to suggest a suitable inscription for the stone lintel over the doors of the new home of the philosophy department.

After some reflection, James sent Eliot a line from the Greek philosopher Protagoras: "Man is the measure of all things."

James never heard back from Eliot, so his curiosity was piqued when he spotted artisans working on a scaffold hidden by a canvas. One morning the scaffold and canvas were gone. The inscription? "What is man that thou art mindful of him?"

Eliot had replaced James's suggestion with words from the Psalmist. Between these two lines lies the great distance between the God-centered and the human-centered points of view.

—Warren Bird
(God's Love, Humanism)

Dates used:_____

Thomas Aquinas, the famous medieval theologian, created one of the greatest intellectual achievements of Western civilization in his *Summa Theologica.* It's a massive work: thirty-eight treatises, three thousand articles, ten thousand objections. Thomas tried to gather into one coherent whole all of truth. What an undertaking: anthropology, science, ethics, psychology, political theory, and theology, all under God.

On December 6, 1273, Thomas abruptly stopped his work. While celebrating Mass in the Chapel of St. Thomas, he caught a glimpse of eternity, and suddenly he knew that all his efforts to describe God fell so far short that he decided never to write again.

When his secretary, Reginald, tried to encourage him to do more writing, he said, "Reginald, I can do no more. Such things have been revealed to me that all I have written seems as so much straw."

Even the greatest human minds cannot fathom the greatness of God.

—Don McCullough
(Human Limitations, Insignificance)

Dates used:_____

God's Nature

Recently, third and fourth-graders at Wheaton (IL) Christian Grammar School were asked to complete the following sentence: "By faith, I know that God is . . .

- "forgiving, because he forgave in the Bible, and he forgave me when I went in the road on my bike without one of my parents" (Amanda)
- "providingful, because he dropped manna for Moses and the people, and he gave my dad a job" (Brandon)
- "caring, because he made the blind man see, and he made me catch a very fast line drive that could have hurt me. He probably sent an angel down" (Paul)
- "merciful, because my brother has been nice to me for a year" (Jeremy)
- "faithful, because the school bill came, and my mom didn't know how we were going to pay it. Two minutes later, my dad called, and he just got a bonus check. My mom was in tears" (anonymous)
- "sweet, because he gave me a dog. God tells me not to do things that are bad. I need someone like that" (Hannah).

—*Cornerstone* Newsletter
(Children, Insight)

Dates used:_____

In *Directions,* James Hamilton writes:

Before refrigerators, people used ice houses to preserve their food. Ice houses had thick walls, no windows, and a tightly fitted door. In winter, when streams and lakes were frozen, large blocks of ice were cut, hauled to the ice houses, and covered with sawdust. Often the ice would last well into the summer.

One man lost a valuable watch while working in an ice house. He searched diligently for it, carefully raking through the sawdust, but didn't find it. His fellow workers also looked, but their efforts, too, proved futile. A small boy who heard about the fruitless search slipped into the ice house during the noon hour and soon emerged with the watch.

Amazed, the men asked him how he found it.

"I closed the door," the boy replied, "lay down in the sawdust, and kept very still. Soon I heard the watch ticking."

Often the question is not whether God is speaking, but whether we are being still enough, and quiet enough, to hear.

—Phillip Gunter
(Listening, Solitude)

Dates used:_____

Grace

David Seamands ends his book *Healing Grace* with this story:

For more than six hundred years the Hapsburgs exercised political power in Europe. When Emperor Franz-Josef I of Austria died in 1916, his was the last of the extravagant imperial funerals.

A processional of dignitaries and elegantly dressed court personages escorted the coffin, draped in the black-and-gold imperial colors. To the accompaniment of a military band's somber dirges and by the light of torches, the cortege descended the stairs of the Capuchin Monastery in Vienna. At the bottom was a great iron door leading to the Hapsburg family crypt. Behind the door was the Cardinal-Archbishop of Vienna.

The officer in charge followed the prescribed ceremony, established centuries before. "Open!" he cried.

"Who goes there?" responded the Cardinal.

"We bear the remains of his Imperial and Apostolic Majesty, Franz-Josef I, by the grace of God Emperor of Austria, King of Hungary, Defender of the Faith, Prince of Bohemia-Moravia, Grand Duke of Lombardy, Venezia, Styrgia . . ." The officer continued to list the Emperor's thirty-seven titles.

"We know him not," replied the Cardinal. "Who goes there?"

The officer spoke again, this time using a much abbreviated and less ostentatious title reserved for times of expediency.

"We know him not," the Cardinal said again.

"Who goes there?"

The officer tried a third time, stripping the emperor of all but the humblest of titles: "We bear the body of Franz-Josef, our brother, a sinner like us all!"

At that, the doors swung open, and Franz-Josef was admitted.

In death, all are reduced to the same level. Neither wealth nor fame can open the way of salvation, but only God's grace, given to those who will humbly acknowledge their need.

—Alan J. White
(Humility, Power)

Dates used:_____

Grace

Overseas Crusades International missionary Chuck Holsinger relates the following experience of one of his Wheaton College classmates:

It was 1944 and my friend, Bert Frizen, was an infantryman on the front lines in Europe. American forces had advanced in the face of intermittent shelling and small-arms fire throughout the morning hours, but now all was quiet. His patrol reached the edge of a wooded area with an open field before them. Unbeknownst to the Americans, a battery of Germans was ready and waiting in a hedgerow about two hundred yards across the field.

Bert was one of the two scouts who moved out into the clearing. Once he was half-way across the field, the remainder of his battalion followed. Suddenly the Germans opened fire and machine gun fire ripped into both of Bert's legs. The American battalion withdrew into the woods for protection, while a rapid exchange of fire continued.

Bert lay helplessly in a small stream as shots volleyed overhead from side to side. There seemed to be no way out of his dilemma. To make matters worse, he now noticed that a German soldier was crawling toward him. Death appeared imminent; he closed his eyes and waited. To his surprise, a considerable period passed without the expected attack, so he ventured opening his eyes again. He was startled to see the German kneeling at his side, smiling. He then noticed that the shooting had stopped. Troops from both sides of the battlefield watched anxiously. Without any verbal exchange, this mysterious

German reached down to lift Bert in his strong arms, and proceeded to carry him to the safety of his own comrades.

Having accomplished his self-appointed mission, and still without speaking a word, the German soldier turned and walked back across the field to his own troop. No one dared break the silence of this sacred moment. Moments later the cease-fire ended, but not before all those present had witnessed the power of self-abdicating love, how one man risked everything for his enemy.

Bert's life was saved through the compassion of one man, his enemy. This courageous act pictures what Jesus risked for us: "While we were still God's enemies, Christ died for us" (Rom. 5:8).

—Lynn McAdam
(Mercy, War)

Dates used:_____

Grace

Actor Kevin Bacon recounted when his 6-year-old son saw *Footloose* for the first time:

He said, "Hey, Dad, you know that thing in the movie where you swing from the rafters of that building? That's really cool, how did you do that?"

I said, "Well, I didn't do that part . . . it was a stunt man."

"What's a stunt man?" he asked.

"That's someone who dresses like me and does things I can't do."

"Oh," he replied and walked out of the room looking a little confused.

A little later he said, "Hey, Dad, you know that thing in the movie where you spin around on that gym bar and land on your feet? How did you do that?"

I said, "Well, I didn't do that. It was a gymnastics double."

"What's a gymnastics double?" he asked.

"That's a guy who dresses in my clothes and does things I can't do."

There was silence from my son, then he asked in a concerned voice, "Dad, what *did* you do?"

"I got all the glory," I sheepishly replied.

That's the grace of God in our lives. Jesus took our sin upon himself and did what we couldn't do. We stand forgiven and bask sheepishly triumphant in Jesus' glory.

—Joel Sarrault
(Credit, Glory)

Dates used:_____

An engagement ring that fell into the sea off the west coast of Sweden in 1994 miraculously found its way back to its owner. The ring was consumed by a mussel that turned up in a load of shellfish caught by fisherman Peder Carlsson.

Carlsson was able to return the ring to its owner because the woman, Agneta Wingstedt, had her name engraved on the inside.

If we bear Christ's name, we know we'll be returned to him one day.

—*Parade Magazine* (12/26/96)
(Heaven, Marriage)

Dates used:_____

Grace

Reader's Digest told of the late Harvey Penick: In the 1920s Penick bought a red spiral notebook and began jotting down observations about golf. He never showed the book to anyone except his son until 1991, when he shared it with a local writer and asked if he thought it was worth publishing. The man read it and told him yes. He left word with Penick's wife the next evening that Simon & Schuster had agreed to an advance of $90,000.

When the writer saw Penick later, the old man seemed troubled. Finally, Penick came clean. With all his medical bills, he said, there was no way he could advance Simon & Schuster that much money. The writer had to explain that Penick would be the one to receive the $90,000.

His first golf book, *Harvey Penick's Little Red Book,* sold more than a million copies, one of the biggest in the history of sports books. His second book, *And If You Play Golf, You're My Friend,* sold nearly three-quarters of a million.

People often have Penick's reaction to the fabulous gift of salvation offered in Jesus Christ. We ask, "What must I do?"

God answers, "Just receive."

—Eric Hulstrand
(Gift, Salvation)

Dates used:_____

Mother Theresa told this story in an address at the National Prayer Breakfast in 1994:

One evening we went out, and we picked up four people from the street. One of them was in a most terrible condition. I told the sisters, "You take care of the other three; I will take care of the one who looks the worst." So I did for her all that my love could do. I put her in bed, and there was such a beautiful smile on her face. She took hold of my hand as she said two words only: "Thank you." Then she died.

I could not help but examine my conscience before her. *What would I say if I were in her place?* My answer was very simple. I would have tried to draw a little attention to myself. I would have said, "I am hungry, I am dying, I am in pain," or something. But she gave me much more; she gave me her grateful love. And she died with a smile on her face.

Gratitude brings a smile and becomes a gift.

(Death, Ministry)

Dates used:_____

Gratitude

An article in the *National Geographic* (9/91) tells of a young man from Hanover, Pennsylvania, who was badly burned in a boiler explosion. To save his life, physicians covered him with 6,000 square centimeters of donor skin, as well as sheets of skin cultured from a stamp-sized piece of his own unburned skin.

A journalist asked him, "Do you ever think about the donor who saved you?"

The young man replied, "To be alive because of a dead donor is too big, too much, so I don't think about it."

Difficult to do, yes, but Christians have also received a similar gift—overwhelming, and worth thinking about.

—Bob Kapler
(Recognition, Sacrifice)

Dates used:_____

I n *The New Yorker* (5/15/95), Sara Mosle recounts that on March 18, 1937, a spark ignited a cloud of natural gas that had accumulated in the basement of the London, Texas, school. The blast killed 293 people, most of them children.

"The explosion happened because the local school board wanted to cut heating costs. Natural gas, the by-product of petroleum extraction, was siphoned from a neighboring oil company's pipeline to fuel the building's furnace free of charge.

"London never recovered from the blast that turned the phrase 'boom town' into a bitter joke. The one positive effect of this disastrous event was government regulation requiring companies to add an odorant to natural gas. The distinctive aroma is now so familiar that we often forget natural gas is naturally odorless."

There is a tendency these days to classify all feelings of guilt as hazardous to our self-esteem. In reality, guilt can be valuable, an "odorant" that warns us of danger.

(Consequences, Shortcuts)

Dates used:_____

Guilt

In 1980 a Boston court acquitted Michael Tindall of flying illegal drugs into the United States. Tindall's attorneys argued that he was a victim of "action addict syndrome," an emotional disorder that makes a person crave dangerous, thrilling situations. Tindall was not a drug dealer, merely a thrill seeker.

An Oregon man who tried to kill his ex-wife was acquitted on the grounds that he suffered from "depression/suicide syndrome," whose victims deliberately commit poorly planned crimes with the unconscious goal of being caught or killed. He didn't really want to shoot his wife; he wanted the police to shoot him.

Then there's the famous "Twinkie syndrome." Attorneys for Dan White, who murdered San Francisco mayor George Moscone, blamed the crime on emotional stress linked to White's junk food binges. White was acquitted of murder and convicted on a lesser charge of manslaughter.

Nowadays, nobody's at fault for anything. We are a nation of victims.

—Louis Lotz
(Blame, Fault)

Dates used:_____

No professional football team that plays its home games in a domed stadium with artificial turf has ever won the Super Bowl.

While a climate-controlled stadium protects players (and fans) from the misery of sleet, snow, mud, heat, and wind, players who brave the elements on a regular basis are disciplined to handle hardship wherever it's found. The Green Bay Packers were the 1996 Super Bowl champions, in part, because of the discipline gained from regularly playing in some of the worst weather in the country.

"Endure hardship as discipline. . . . No discipline seems pleasant at the time, but painful. Later on, however, it produces a harvest of righteousness and peace for those who have been trained by it" (Heb. 12:7, 11).

—Greg Asimakoupoulos
(Discipline, Training)

Dates used:_____

Harmony

The *Atlantic Monthly* (11/94) told about superstar tenors Jose Carreras, Placido Domingo, and Luciano Pavarotti performing together in Los Angeles. A reporter tried to press the issue of competitiveness between the three men.

"You have to put all of your concentration into opening your heart to the music," Domingo said. "You can't be rivals when you're together making music."

That's also true in the church.

(Rivalry, Teamwork)

Dates used:_____

When Charles V stepped down as the Holy
Roman Emperor some 400 years ago, he spent
much of his time at his palace in Spain. He had six
clocks there, and no matter how he tried, he could
never get them to chime together on the hour.

In his memoirs he wrote, "How is it possible for
six different clocks to chime all at the same time?
How is it even more impossible for the six nations of
the Holy Roman Empire to live in harmony? It can't
be done. It's impossible, even if they call themselves
Christians."

Today, we know it's possible to have clocks in
perfect harmony, when all are powered by the same
source and all are calibrated to the same standard—
Greenwich Mean Time. Likewise, unity in the church
is possible, but only when all are calibrated to one
standard—Christ.

—Wayne Brouwer
Preaching Today
(Cooperation, Unity)

Dates used:_____

Heart

In September 1993, with the Major League Baseball season nearing its end, the first-place Philadelphia Phillies visited the second-place Montreal Expos.

In the first game of the series, the home team Expos came to bat one inning, trailing 7–4. Their first two batters reached base. The manager sent a pinch hitter to the plate, rookie Curtis Pride, who had never gotten a hit in the major leagues. Pride took his warm-up swings, walked to the plate, and on the first pitch laced a double, scoring two runners.

The stadium thundered as 45,757 fans screamed their approval. The Expos third base coach called time, walked toward Pride, and told him to take off his batting helmet.

What's wrong with my helmet? wondered the rookie. Then, realizing what his coach meant, Pride tipped his cap to the appreciative fans.

After the game, someone asked Pride if he could hear the cheering. This person wasn't giving the rookie a hard time. Curtis Pride is 95 percent deaf.

"Here," Pride said, pointing to his heart. "I could hear it here."

Sometimes we hear things loudest in our hearts.

—Harry J. Heintz
(Approval, Celebration)

Dates used:_____

Annie Dillard, in her book *Pilgrim at Tinker Creek,* writes:

At the end of the island I noticed a small green frog. He was exactly half in and half out of the water.

He was a very small frog with wide, dull eyes. And just as I looked at him, he slowly crumpled and began to sag. The spirit vanished from his eyes as if snuffed. His skin emptied and drooped; his very skull seemed to collapse and settle like a kicked tent. . . .

An oval shadow hung in the water behind the drained frog: then the shadow glided away. The frog skin bag started to sink.

I had read about the water bug, but never seen one. "Giant water bug" is really the name of the creature, which is an enormous, heavy-bodied brown beetle. It eats insects, tadpoles, fish, and frogs. Its grasping forelegs are mighty and hooked inward. It seizes a victim with these legs, hugs it tight, and paralyzes it with enzymes injected during a vicious bite. Through the puncture shoots the poison that dissolves the victim's muscles and bones and organs—all but the skin—and through it the giant water bug sucks out the victim's body, reduced to juice.

Hidden sins can suck the life out of us.

—Dave Goetz
(Satan, Sin's Penalty)

Dates used:_____

Holy Spirit

In the book *Healing the Masculine Soul,* Gordon Dalbey says that when Jesus refers to the Holy Spirit as the Helper, he uses a Greek word, *paraclete,* that was an ancient warrior's term.

"Greek soldiers went into battle in pairs," says Dalbey, "so when the enemy attacked, they could draw together back-to-back, covering each other's blind side. One's battle partner was the *paraclete.*"

Our Lord does not send us to fight the good fight alone. The Holy Spirit is our battle partner who covers our blind side and fights for our well being.

—Tom Tripp
(Help, Support)

Dates used:_____

Pastor John B. McGarvey tells this story:
One day our church copier broke down. I'm not mechanically minded, but I called the repair shop to see if they could tell me what the problem was and if I could do anything about it. I quickly discovered, however, that I didn't even know how to describe what was broken. I didn't know the names of the parts or what was specifically wrong. I just knew the copy machine didn't work.

So the repair shop sent out a technician. While working on our machine, he also called the shop. Unlike me, he knew how to describe what was needed. He used words I didn't understand, but the person at the shop did, and soon the copier was repaired.

My need was met because someone came and communicated to headquarters in words I could not express. The apostle Paul teaches in Romans 8 that this is what the Holy Spirit does for us. When we don't know how to pray, the Holy Spirit knows precisely what we need and prays in a language the Father perfectly understands.

(Intercession, Prayer)

Dates used:_____

Honesty

Charles Swindoll, in *Growing Deep in the Christian Life,* tells about a man who bought fried chicken dinners for himself and his date late one afternoon. The attendant at the fast food outlet, however, inadvertently gave him the proceeds from the day's business—a bucket of money (much of it cash) instead of fried chicken. Swindoll writes:

After driving to their picnic site, the two of them sat down to enjoy some chicken. They discovered a whole lot more than chicken—over $800! But he was unusual. He quickly put the money back in the bag. They got back into the car and drove all the way back. By then, the manager was frantic.

Mr. Clean got out, walked in, and became an instant hero. "I want you to know I came by to get a couple of chicken dinners and wound up with all this money here."

Well, the manager was thrilled to death. He said, "Let me call the newspaper. I'm gonna have your picture put in the local paper. You're one of the most honest men I've ever heard of."

To which the man quickly responded, "Oh, no. No, no, don't do that!" Then he leaned closer and whispered, "You see, the woman I'm with . . . she's, uh, somebody else's wife."

One can be honest and still not have integrity.

—Phillip Gunter
(Infidelity, Integrity)

Dates used:_____

A little honesty paid handsome dividends for Herbert Tarvin, 11, who drew praise for returning eighty-five cents that he picked up after an armored car crashed and spilled hundreds of thousands of dollars on a Miami street. For his honesty, Herbert, his family, and his sixth-grade class at St. Francis Xavier Catholic School spent the day at Walt Disney World in Orlando, Florida, on the tab of Disney and Southwest Airlines. Herbert said he had to "do the right thing and turn the money in because it doesn't belong to me."

Police say more than $500,000 is still missing. Only a single mother of six, who turned in about $20 in quarters and pennies, and Herbert returned the money, officials said.

—USA Today (2/14/97)
(Integrity, Rewards)

Dates used:_____

Honesty

Coming home from work, a woman stopped at the corner deli to buy a chicken for supper. The butcher reached into a barrel, grabbed the last chicken he had, flung it on the scales behind the counter, and told the woman its weight.

She thought for a moment. "I really need a bit more chicken than that," she said. "Do you have any larger ones?"

Without a word, the butcher put the chicken back into the barrel, groped around as though finding another, pulled the same chicken out, and placed it on the scales. "This chicken weighs one pound more," he announced.

The woman pondered her options and then said, "Okay. I'll take them both."

Deceit is detected sooner or later.

—Clark Cothern
(Deceit, Guile)

Dates used:_____

In October 1864, word came to President Abraham Lincoln of a Mrs. Bixby, a Boston widow whose five sons had all been killed fighting in the Civil War. Lincoln later wrote his condolences:

Dear Madam,

I have been shown in the files of the War Department a statement of the Adjutant General of Massachusetts that you are the mother of five sons who have died gloriously on the field of battle.

I feel how weak and fruitless must be any word mine which should attempt to beguile you from the grief of loss so overwhelming. But I cannot refrain from tendering you the consolation that may be found in the thanks of the republic they died to save.

I pray that our heavenly Father may assuage the anguish of your bereavement, and leave you only the cherished memory of the loved and lost, and the solemn pride that must be yours to have laid so costly a sacrifice upon the altar of freedom.

Yours very sincerely and respectfully,

Abraham Lincoln.

How beautiful the story would be if it ended here with the simple, literary elegance that was Lincoln's alone. But the story took an ironic turn just a few weeks after the letter was sent. No sooner had Mrs. Bixby received her letter when it was leaked to the press by someone in the White House. It was proclaimed a masterpiece for some weeks until a reporter went to the records of the Adjutant General and discovered that the President had been given bad information.

(continued)

Honor

(continued)

Mrs. Bixby had not lost all five of her sons in battle. One was killed in action at Fredericksburg. One was killed in action at Petersburg. One was taken prisoner at Gettysburg and later exchanged and returned to his mother in good health. One deserted to the enemy. One deserted his post and fled the country.

Word got out, and the press, as well as the rest of the Union, became divided in its support of the President. Some said he had been innocently duped. Others said his feelings were sincere if the cause was not.

Carl Sandburg, in his exhaustive biography of Lincoln, has the last word:

"Whether all five had died on the field of battle, or only two, four of her sons had been poured away into the river of war. The two who had deserted were as lost to her as though dead. The one who had returned had fought at Gettysburg. . . . She deserved some kind of token, some award approaching the language Lincoln had employed. Lincoln was not deceived."

How like the Bixby family is each one of us: a mixture of success and failure, honor and shame. Yet, knowing the whole story of our lives, Christ will honor those who serve him.

—Dean Feldmeyer
(Deception, War)

Dates used:_____

As vice president, George Bush represented the United States at the funeral of former Soviet leader Leonid Brezhnev. Bush was deeply moved by a silent protest carried out by Brezhnev's widow. She stood motionless by the coffin until seconds before it was closed. Then, just as the soldiers touched the lid, Brezhnev's wife performed an act of great courage and hope, a gesture that must surely rank as one of the most profound acts of civil disobedience ever committed: She reached down and made the sign of the cross on her husband's chest.

There, in the citadel of secular, atheistic power, the wife of the man who had run it all hoped that her husband was wrong. She hoped that there was another life, and that that life was best represented by Jesus who died on the cross, and that the same Jesus might yet have mercy on her husband.

—Gary Thomas
Christianity Today (10/3/94)
(Civil Disobedience, Faith)

Dates used:_____

When complimented on her homemade biscuits, the cook at a popular Christian conference center told Dr. Harry Ironside, "Just consider what goes into the making of these biscuits. The flour itself doesn't taste good, neither does the baking powder, nor the shortening, nor the other ingredients. However, when I mix them all together and put them in the oven, they come out just right."

Much of life seems tasteless, even bad, but God is able to combine these ingredients of our life in such a way that a banquet results.

—Greg Asimakoupoulos
(Circumstance, Providence)

Dates used:_____

In 1994, Thurman Thomas, head bowed with his hands covering his face, sat on the Buffalo Bills bench following his team's fourth straight Super Bowl loss. His three fumbles had helped seal their awful fate.

Suddenly, standing before him was the Dallas Cowboys' star running back, Emmitt Smith. Just named MVP for Super Bowl XXVIII, Smith was carrying his small goddaughter. Smith looked down at her and said, "I want you to meet the greatest running back in the NFL, Mr. Thurman Thomas."

Paul tells us, "In humility consider others better than yourselves" (Phil. 2:3).

—Allen Mann
(Recognition, Reputation)

Dates used:_____

Identity

In the town of Stepanavan, Armenia, I met a woman whom everyone called "Palasan's Wife." She had her own name, of course, but townspeople called her by her husband's name to show her great honor.

When the devastating 1988 earthquake struck Armenia, it was nearly noon, and Palasan was at work. He rushed to the elementary school where his son was a student. The facade was already crumbling, but he entered the building and began pushing children outside to safety. After Palasan had managed to help twenty-eight children out, an aftershock hit that completely collapsed the school building and killed him.

So the people of Stepanavan honor his memory and his young widow by calling her Palasan's wife.

Sometimes a person's greatest honor is not who he or she is but to whom he or she is related. The highest honor of any believer is to be called a disciple of Jesus Christ, who laid down his life for all people.

—L. Nishan Bakalian
(Discipleship, Sacrifice)

Dates used:_____

In 1990, center fielder Brett Butler left the San Franciso Giants as a free agent, joining the cross-state rivals, the Los Angeles Dodgers. When Butler returned to San Francisco for the first time as a Los Angeles Dodger, Giant fans greeted him with a mix of boos and cheers.

The cheers turned to boos, however, when Butler hugged Los Angeles manager Tommy Lasorda. "It turned a page in my career," said Butler. "I'm an L.A. Dodger now; I'm not a Giant. That just kind of solidified it. I wanted them to know, I'm a Dodger."

When people become Christians, in one way or another they need to identify with Jesus in the sight of all their family, friends, and acquaintances.

—Richard C. Kauffman, Jr.
(Baptism, Witness)

Dates used:_____

Incarnation

On March 5, 1994, Deputy Sheriff Lloyd Prescott was teaching a class for police officers in the Salt Lake City Library. As he stepped into the hallway he noticed a gunman herding eighteen hostages into the next room. Dressed in street clothes, Prescott joined the group as the nineteenth hostage, followed them into the room, and shut the door. When the gunman announced the order in which hostages would be executed, Prescott identified himself as a cop. In the scuffle that followed, Prescott, in self-defense, fatally shot the armed man. The hostages were released unharmed.

God dressed in street clothes and entered our world, joining those held hostage to sin. On the cross Jesus defeated Satan and set us free from the power of sin.

—Greg Asimakoupoulos
(Sacrifice, Salvation)

Dates used:_____

Joe Torre had been a catcher and a broadcast announcer for the St. Louis Cardinals. Shortly after he was named manager, according to the *Pittsburgh Press*, New York Yankees' announcer Phil Rizzuto suggested that managing could be done better from high above the baseball field—from the level of the broadcasting booth.

Torre replied, "Upstairs, you can't look in their eyes."

In Jesus Christ, God also chose to come down on the field and look into our eyes.

—David R. Martin
(Identification, Viewpoint)

Dates used:_____

Incarnation

Joseph Damien was a nineteenth-century missionary who ministered to people with leprosy on the island of Molokai, Hawaii. Those suffering grew to love him and revered the sacrificial life he lived out before them.

One morning before Damien was to lead daily worship, he was pouring some hot water into a cup when the water swirled out and fell onto his bare foot. It took him a moment to realize that he had not felt any sensation. Gripped by the sudden fear of what this could mean, he poured more hot water on the same spot. No feeling whatsoever.

Damien immediately knew what had happened. As he walked tearfully to deliver his sermon, no one at first noticed the difference in his opening line. He normally began every sermon with, "My fellow believers." But this morning he began with, "My fellow lepers."

In a greater measure Jesus came into this world knowing what it would cost him. He bore in his pure being the marks of evil, that we might be made pure. "For this I came into the world," (John 18:37).

—Ravi Zacharias in *Deliver Us From Evil*
(Identification, Solidarity)

Dates used:_____

John Howard Griffin was a white man who believed he could never understand the plight of African-Americans unless he became like one. In 1959, he darkened his skin with medication, sun lamps, and stains, then traveled throughout the South. His book, *Black Like Me,* helped whites better understand the humiliation and discrimination faced daily by people of color.

Jesus Christ became like us; the Incarnation is evidence that God understands our plight. "He was despised and rejected by men, a man of sorrows, and familiar with suffering" (Isa. 53:3).

—Tom Moorhouse
(Identity, Racial Reconciliation)

Dates used:_____

Indifference

An estimated 500,000 tons of water rush over Niagara Falls every minute. On March 29, 1948, the falls suddenly stopped. People living within the sound of the falls were awakened by the overwhelming silence. They believed it was a sign that the world was coming to an end. It was thirty hours before the rush of water resumed.

What happened? Heavy winds had set the ice fields of Lake Erie in motion. Tons of ice jammed the Niagara River entrance near Buffalo and stopped the flow of the river until the ice shifted again.

The flow of God's grace in our lives can be blocked by cold indifference.

—Merle Mees
(Grace, Sin)

Dates used:_____

Mezzo-soprano Susan Graham is one of opera's rising young stars. In a profile for *Texas Monthly* (12/96), writer Jamie Schilling Fields sought to compare Graham with one of opera's legendary mezzo-sopranos, and asked if she could be the next Cecilia Bartoli.

Graham asserted, "I'm not sure I want to be the next *anyone*. I'd rather be the first Susan Graham."

(Comparison, Confidence)

Dates used:_____

Integrity

Scientists now say that a series of slits, not a giant gash, sank the *Titanic*.

The opulent, 900-foot cruise ship sank in 1912 on its first voyage, from England to New York. Fifteen hundred people died in the worst maritime disaster of the time.

The most widely held theory is that the ship hit an iceberg, which opened a huge gash in the side of the liner. But an international team of divers and scientists recently used sound waves to probe through the wreckage, buried in mud two-and-a-half miles deep. Their discovery? The damage was surprisingly small. Instead of the huge gash, they found six relatively narrow slits across the six watertight holds. "Everything that could go wrong did," said William Garzke, Jr., a naval architect who helped the team with their analysis.

Small damage, below the water line and invisible to most, can sink a huge ship. In the same way, small compromises, unseen to others, can ultimately sink a person's character.

—*USA Today* (4/9/97)
(Character, Reputation)

Dates used:_____

Don McCullough, president of San Francisco Seminary told this story:

Scottish Presbyterians established churches in Ghana over a hundred years ago, and today their worship services still resemble a formal Scottish Presbyterian service. Recently, however, they have allowed traditional African expressions into the worship service.

Now the people dance as they bring their offerings forward. The music plays, and each individual joyfully dances down the aisle to the offering plate. According to the missionary to Ghana who told me this, the offering is the only time in the service when the people smile.

No doubt, God also smiles.

(Missions, Stewardship)

Dates used:_____

Legacy

In his book *I Almost Missed the Sunset,* Bill Gaither writes:

Gloria and I had been married a couple of years. We were teaching school in Alexandria, Indiana, where I had grown up, and we wanted a piece of land where we could build a house. I noticed the parcel south of town where cattle grazed, and I learned it belonged to a 92-year-old retired banker named Mr. Yule. He owned a lot of land in the area, and He gave the same speech to everyone who inquired: "I promised the farmers they could use it for their cattle."

Gloria and I visited him at the bank. Although he was retired, he spent a couple of hours each morning in his office. He looked at us over the top of his bifocals.

I introduced myself and told him we were interested in a piece of his land. "Not selling," he said pleasantly. "Promised it to a farmer for grazing."

"I know, but we teach school here and thought maybe you'd be interested in selling it to someone planning to settle in the area."

He pursed his lips and stared at me. "What'd you say your name was?"

"Gaither. Bill Gaither."

"Hmmm. Any relation to Grover Gaither?"

"Yes, sir. He was my granddad."

Mr. Yule put down his paper and removed his glasses. "Interesting. Grover Gaither was the best worker I ever had on my farm. Full day's work for a day's pay. So honest. What'd you say you wanted?"

I told him again.

"Let me do some thinking on it, then come back and see me."

I came back within the week, and Mr. Yule told me he had had the property appraised. I held my breath. "How does $3,800 sound? Would that be okay?"

If that was per acre, I would have to come up with nearly $60,000! "$3,800?" I repeated.

"Yup. Fifteen acres for $3,800."

I knew it had to be worth at least three times that. I readily accepted.

Nearly three decades later, my son and I strolled that beautiful, lush property that had once been pasture land. "Benjy," I said, "you've had this wonderful place to grow up through nothing that you've done, but because of the good name of a great-granddad you never met."

"A good name is more desirable than great riches; to be esteemed is better than silver or gold" (Prov. 22:1).

(*Character, Reputation*)

Dates used:_____

Legalism

The following hand-lettered signs were prominently displayed around a drive-in restaurant in Pine Grove, California:

Do not back in

Restrooms are for customer use only

(On trash can) Not for diaper disposal or auto trash

Local checks for amount of purchase only

Vanilla frosties only dipped one size only

Please order by number

Observe all signs.

"Christ is the end of the law so that there may be righteousness for everyone who believes" (Rom. 10:4).

—Phillip W. Gunter
(Grace, Law)

Dates used:_____

Lee Strobel, teaching pastor at Willow Creek Community Church in South Barrington, Illinois, offers a unique perspective on life in the nineties:

If you really are a person of the 90's. . .

You feel like life is whizzing past you at 90 miles an hour. You work 90 hours a week, and you've still got 90 items on your to-do list. You're on a 90-calorie-a-day diet because you look 90 pounds over-weight in your swimming suit.

You've got 90 different bills to pay, and you're already $90 overdrawn—and that's just the interest. You're still paying $90 a month on your student loan, and you don't know where you're going to get $90,000 to send your kids to school.

You've got 90 channels of cable television, and there is still nothing worth watching. You drive your kids to 90 different activities and events a month. Your toddler just asked "Why?" for the 90th time today.

And you think everything would be fine, if you were just making 90 grand a year.

—Wayne Rouse
(Perspective, Stress)

Dates used:_____

Listening

In his book *Stress Fractures,* Charles Swindoll writes:

I vividly remember some time back being caught in the undertow of too many commitments in too few days. It wasn't long before I was snapping at my wife and our children, choking down my food at mealtimes, and feeling irritated at those unexpected interruptions through the day. Before long, things around our home started reflecting the pattern of my hurry-up style. It was becoming unbearable.

I distinctly recall after supper one evening the words of our younger daughter, Colleen. She wanted to tell me about something important that had happened to her at school that day. She hurriedly began, "Daddy-I-wanna-tell-you-somethin'-and-I'll-tell-you-really-fast."

Suddenly realizing her frustration, I answered, "Honey, you can tell me . . . and you don't have to tell me really fast. Say it slowly."

I'll never forget her answer: "Then listen slowly."

—Mike Schafer
(Hurry, Stress)

Dates used:_____

The German philosopher Schopenhauer compared the human race to a bunch of porcupines huddling together on a cold winter's night. He said, "The colder it gets outside, the more we huddle together for warmth; but the closer we get to one another, the more we hurt one another with our sharp quills. And in the lonely night of earth's winter eventually we begin to drift apart and wander out on our own and freeze to death in our loneliness."

Christ has given us an alternative: to forgive each other for the pokes we receive. That allows us to stay together and stay warm.

—Wayne Brouwer
Preaching Today
(Forgiveness, Relationships)

Dates used:_____

Longevity

After winning the gold medal for the long jump in the 1996 Olympic games, Carl Lewis was asked by Bryant Gumbel on *The Today Show:* "You have competed for almost 20 years. To what do you attribute your longevity?"

Lewis, perhaps the greatest track and field athlete of all time, did not hesitate with his answer: "Remembering that you have both wins and losses along the way. Don't take either one too seriously."

—Sherman L. Burford
(Failure, Success)

Dates used:_____

Lee Iacocca once asked legendary football coach Vince Lombardi what it took to make a winning team. The book *Iacocca* records Lombardi's answer:

There are a lot of coaches with good ball clubs who know the fundamentals and have plenty of discipline but still don't win the game. Then you come to the third ingredient: if you're going to play together as a team, you've got to care for one another. You've got to love each other. Each player has to be thinking about the next guy and saying to himself: *If I don't block that man, Paul is going to get his legs broken. I have to do my job well in order that he can do his.*

"The difference between mediocrity and greatness," Lombardi said that night, "is the feeling these guys have for each other."

In the healthy church, each Christian learns to care for others. As we take seriously Jesus' command to love one another, we contribute to a winning team.

—Christopher Stinnett
(Caregiving, Teamwork)

Dates used:_____

Love

This story comes from a Sunday school ministry in the part of New York City that has been rated the "most likely place to get killed." Pastor Bill Wilson has been stabbed twice, shot at, and had a member of his team killed:

One Puerto Rican lady, after getting saved in church, came to me with an urgent request. She didn't speak a word of English, so she told me through an interpreter, "I want to do something for God, please."

"I don't know what you can do," I answered.

"Please, let me do something," she said in Spanish.

"Okay. I'll put you on a bus. Ride a different bus every week and just love the kids."

So every week she rode a different bus—we have fifty of them—and loved the children. She would find the worst-looking kid on the bus, put him on her lap, and whisper over and over the only words she had learned in English: "I love you. Jesus loves you."

After several months, she became attached to one little boy in particular. "I don't want to change buses anymore. I want to stay on this one bus," she said.

The boy didn't speak. He came to Sunday school every week with his sister and sat on the woman's lap, but he never made a sound. Each week she would tell him all the way to Sunday school and all the way home, "I love you and Jesus loves you."

One day, to her amazement, the little boy turned around and stammered, "I—I love you, too." Then he put his arms around her and gave her a big hug.

That was 2:30 on a Saturday afternoon. At 6:30

that night, the boy was found dead in a garbage bag under a fire escape. His mother had beaten him to death and thrown his body in the trash.

"I love you and Jesus loves you." Those were some of the last words he heard in his short life—from the lips of a Puerto Rican woman who could barely speak English.

Who among us is qualified to minister? Who among us even knows what to do? Not you; not me. But I ran to an altar once, and I got some fire and just went.

So did this woman who couldn't speak English. And so can you.

—Bill Wilson
Charisma (10/96)
(Commitment, Service)

Dates used:_____

Love

In the prologue to *Leadership Jazz*, Max DePree writes about his granddaughter, Zoe:

[Zoe] was born prematurely and weighed one pound, seven ounces, so small that my wedding ring could slide up her arm to her shoulder. The neonatologist who first examined her told us that she had a 5 to 10 percent chance of living three days. When Esther and I saw Zoe in her isolette in the neonatal intensive care unit, she had two IVs in her navel, one in her foot, a monitor on each side of her chest, and a respirator tube and a feeding tube in her mouth.

To complicate matters, Zoe's biological father had jumped ship the month before Zoe was born. Realizing this, a wise and caring nurse named Ruth gave me my instructions. "For the next several months, at least, you're the surrogate father. I want you to come to the hospital every day to visit Zoe, and when you come, I want you to rub her body and her legs and arms with the tip of your finger. While you're caressing her, you should tell her over and over how much you love her, because she has to be able to connect your voice to your touch."

God knew that we also needed both his voice and his touch. So he gave us the Word, his Son, and also his body, the church. God's voice and touch say, "I love you."

—Ed Rotz
(Caregiving, Touch)

Dates used:_____

In *One Inch from the Fence,* Wes Seeliger writes:
I have spent long hours in the intensive care waiting room . . . watching with anguished people . . . listening to urgent questions: Will my husband make it? Will my child walk again? How do you live without your companion of thirty years?

The intensive care waiting room is different from any other place in the world. And the people who wait are different. They can't do enough for each other. No one is rude. The distinctions of race and class melt away. A person is a father first, a black man second. The garbage man loves his wife as much as the university professor loves his, and everyone understands this. Each person pulls for everyone else.

In the intensive care waiting room, the world changes. Vanity and pretense vanish. The universe is focused on the doctor's next report. If only it will show improvement. Everyone knows that loving someone else is what life is all about.

Could we learn to love like that if we realized that every day of life is a day in the waiting room?

—Hugh Duncan
(Common Ground, Patience)

Dates used:_____

Lust

The Illinois Department of Natural Resources reports that more than 17,000 deer die each year after being struck by motorists on state highways. According to Paul Shelton, state wildlife director, the peak season for road kills is in late fall.

Why? The bucks are in rut in November. "They're concentrating almost exclusively on reproductive activities," he said, "and are a lot less wary than they normally would be."

Deer aren't the only creatures destroyed by preoccupation with sex.

—Greg Asimakoupoulos
(Preoccupation, Sex)

Dates used:_____

In *Boardroom Reports* (7/5/93), Peter LeVine writes: When the Port Authority of New York and New Jersey ran a help-wanted ad for electricians with expertise at using Sontag connectors, it got 170 responses—even though there is no such thing as a Sontag connector. The Authority ran the ad to find out how many applicants falsify resumes.

(Honesty, Work)

Dates used:_____

Marriage

The space shuttle *Discovery* was grounded recently—not by technical difficulties or lack of government funding, but by woodpeckers. Yellow-shafted flicker woodpeckers found the insulating foam on the shuttle's external fuel tank irresistible material for pecking.

The foam is critical to the shuttle's performance. Without it, ice forms on the tank when it's filled with the super-cold fuel, ice that can break free during liftoff and damage the giant spacecraft. The shuttle was grounded until the damage was repaired.

Marriages are frequently damaged not only by big things—infidelity or abuse or abandonment—but by the little things. Criticism, lack of respect, and taking each other for granted peck away at the relationship and keep us from reaching the heights of love.

(Criticism, Relationships)

Dates used:_____

Finns who can't get enough of winter swarmed to the northern town of Kemi for the opening of a sprawling ice castle that features a theater, a playground, an art gallery, and a chapel.

Thirty workers took three months to build this year's castle with 13-foot walls stretching for 1,650 feet.

"We reckon this must be the world's most popular construction site," castle spokesman Simeoni Sainio said.

An Orthodox Church chapel, hewn from ice, already has been booked for four weddings and a christening. The theater has a capacity of 3,000 and will feature rock and pop concerts, musicals, modern dance, opera recitals and the popular opera "Amahl and the Night Visitors."

Construction and upkeep costs are estimated to be $1.1 million, yet the castle will melt sometime in mid-April.

The melting ice castle is a reminder that all the material things in this world will one day pass away. Let's lay up our treasure in heaven, not on earth (Matt. 6:19–24).

—Scott Wooddell
(Folly, Wealth)

Dates used:_____

Maturity

In *First Things First,* A. Roger Merrill tells of a business consultant who decided to landscape his grounds. He hired a woman with a doctorate in horticulture who was extremely knowledgeable.

Because the business consultant was very busy and traveled a lot, he kept emphasizing to her the need to create his garden in a way that would require little or no maintenance on his part. He insisted on automatic sprinklers and other labor-saving devices.

Finally she stopped and said, "There's one thing you need to deal with before we go any further. If there's no gardener, there's no garden!"

There are no labor-saving devices for growing a garden of spiritual virtue. Becoming a person of spiritual fruitfulness requires time, attention, and care.

—Bill Norman
(Discipleship, Spiritual Growth)

Dates used:_____

A TV news camera crew was on assignment in southern Florida filming the widespread destruction of Hurricane Andrew.

In one scene, amid the devastation and debris stood one house on its foundation. The owner was cleaning up the yard when a reporter approached him.

"Sir, why is your house the only one still standing?" asked the reporter. "How did you manage to escape the severe damage of the hurricane?"

"I built this house myself," the man replied. "I also built it according to the Florida state building code. When the code called for 2 x 6 roof trusses, I used 2 x 6 roof trusses. I was told that a house built according to code could withstand a hurricane. I did, and it did. I suppose no one else around here followed the code."

When the sun is shining and the skies are blue, building our lives on something other than the guidelines in God's Word can be tempting. But there's only one way to be ready for a storm.

—David R. Culver
(Rules, Word of God)

Dates used:_____

Optimism

Craig Randall drives a garbage truck in Peabody, Massachusetts. In a garbage container one day, he noticed a Wendy's soft drink cup bearing a contest sticker. Having won a chicken sandwich the week before, Randall checked it, hoping for some french fries or a soft drink.

Instead, he peeled a sticker worth $200,000 toward the construction of a new home, reports *U.S. News & World Report* (11/6/95).

What we get out of life depends a lot on what we look for. Are we more likely to see each experience as trash or a potential treasure?

—Bob Weniger
(Expectations, Hope)

Dates used:_____

J erry Rice, who plays for football's San Francisco 49ers, is considered by many experts the best receiver in the NFL. Interviewers from Black Entertainment Television once asked Rice, "Why did you attend a small, obscure university like Mississippi Valley State University in Itta Bena, Mississippi?"

Rice responded, "Out of all the big-time schools (such as UCLA) to recruit me, MVSU was the only school to come to my house and give me a personal visit."

The big-time schools sent cards, letters, and advertisements, but only one showed Rice personal attention.

If we want to share our faith, there's still nothing like a personal touch.

—Edward J. Robinson
(Evangelism, Friendship)

Dates used:_____

Past Events

Two Buddhist monks were walking just after a thunderstorm. They came to a swollen stream. A beautiful, young Japanese woman in a kimono stood there wanting to cross to the other side, but she was afraid of the currents.

One of the monks said, "Can I help you?"

"I need to cross this stream," replied the woman.

The monk picked her up, put her on his shoulder, carried her through the swirling waters, and put her down on the other side. He and his companion then went on to the monastery.

That night his companion said to him, "I have a bone to pick with you. As Buddhist monks, we have taken vows not to look on a woman, much less touch her body. Back there by the river you did both."

"My brother," answered the other monk, "I put that woman down on the other side of the river. You're still carrying her in your mind."

How easy it is to be obsessed with the past at the expense of the future.

—John Claypool
(Lust, Temptation)

Dates used:_____

Author John Claypool shares this story:
Years ago a thunderstorm swept through southern Kentucky at the farm where my Claypool forebears have lived for six generations. In the orchard, the wind blew over an old pear tree that had been there as long as anybody could remember. My grandfather was grieved to lose the tree on which he had climbed as a boy and whose fruit he had eaten all his life.

A neighbor came by and said, "Doc, I'm really sorry to see your pear tree blown down."

"I'm sorry too," said my grandfather. "It was a real part of my past."

"What are you going to do?" the neighbor asked.

My grandfather paused for a moment and then said, "I'm going to pick the fruit and burn what's left."

That is the wise way to deal with many things in our past. We need to learn their lessons, enjoy their pleasures, and then go on with the present and the future.

(Memories, Regret)

Dates used:_____

Perfectionism

In a full-page ad in *USA Today*, sports shoe manu-facturer Fila honored its NBA all-star spokesman Grant Hill and, at the same time, took a wry swipe at the pressure young people feel to be perfect. The ad pictures Hill surrounded by this copy:

This year Grant Hill led his team in scoring, rebounding, assists, and steals, led his team back into the playoffs, led the league in triple doubles, led the league in All-Star balloting, earned a place [on the Olympic team] in Atlanta, didn't punch an official, didn't demand a contract extension, was never tardy, was always cordial, didn't dump his high school friends, listened to his mother, remembered the doorman at Christmas, made his bed daily, threw a successful party, . . . promised to take shorter showers in an effort to conserve water, got plenty of sleep, finally fixed that loose brick in the walkway so the mailman wouldn't trip, got to the bottom of it all, didn't hurt a fly, organized his thoughts, chose paper over plastic, appeared fully clothed in most interviews, improved his vocabulary, counted his blessings, rewound tapes before returning them, said nice things about his teammates, fed coins into other people's meters, kept his thermostat at 68, practiced what he preached, actually paid attention to the stewardess's emergency flight instructions, donated a kidney, and vowed to do better next year.

(Fantasy, Overachievement)

Dates used:_____

Jean-Dominique Bauby, 45, a French journalist who had been editor-in-chief of the fashion magazine *Elle*, suffered a stroke in December of 1995. It left him unable to either speak or move, although his mind was unaffected. The only part of his body still left under voluntary control was his left eyelid.

Bauby learned to communicate with that eyelid. First, he learned a signal for "yes" and another for "no." Then when a therapist recited or pointed to the letters in the French alphabet, he would blink when she reached the letter he wanted. In this way, he formed words, then sentences. Difficult though it was, he composed an entire book, *The Diving Suit and the Butterfly*, prior to his death on March 9, 1997. In its first week of publication, it sold 146,000 copies.

Bauby did what he could with what he had. To each of us the Lord has given some ability and some opportunity for service.

—Harry Adams
(Achievement, Determination)

Dates used:_____

Perseverance

Mario Cuomo, former governor of New York, wrote in *Life* about a time when he was especially discouraged during a political campaign:

I couldn't help wondering what Poppa would have said if I told him I was tired or—God forbid—discouraged. A thousand pictures flashed through my mind, but one scene came sharply into view.

We had just moved to Holliswood, New York, from our apartment behind the store. We had our own house for the first time; it had some land around it, even trees. One in particular was a great blue spruce that must have been forty feet tall.

Less than a week after we moved in, there was a terrible storm. We came home from the store that night to find the spruce pulled almost totally from the ground and flung forward, its mighty nose bent in the asphalt of the street. My brother Frankie and I could climb poles all day; we were great at fire escapes; we could scale fences with barbed wire—but we knew nothing about trees. When we saw our spruce, defeated, its cheek on the canvas, our hearts sank. But not Poppa's.

Maybe he was five feet six if his heels were not worn. Maybe he weighed 155 pounds if he had a good meal. Maybe he could see a block away if his glasses were clean. But he was stronger than Frankie and me and Marie and Momma all together. We stood in the street, looking down at the tree.

"Okay, we gonna push 'im up!"

"What are you talking about, Poppa? The roots are out of the ground!"

"Shut up, we gonna push 'im up, he's gonna grow again." You couldn't say no to him. So we followed him into the house and we got what rope there was and we tied the rope around the tip of the tree that lay in the asphalt, and he stood up by the house, with me pulling on the rope and Frankie in the street in the rain, helping to push up the great blue spruce. In no time at all, we had it standing up straight again!

With the rain still falling, Poppa dug away at the place where the roots were, making a muddy hole wider and wider as the tree sank lower and lower toward security. Then we shoveled mud over the roots and moved boulders to the base to keep the tree in place. Poppa drove stakes in the ground, tied rope from the trunk to the stakes, and maybe two hours later looked at the spruce, the crippled spruce made straight by ropes, and said, "Don't worry, he's gonna grow again. . . ."

If you were to drive past that house today, you would see the great, straight blue spruce, maybe sixty-five feet tall, pointing up to the heavens, pretending it never had its nose in the asphalt.

Remembering that night in Holliswood, I now couldn't wait to get back into the campaign.

(Determination, Discouragement)

Dates used:_____

Perseverance

Runner's World (8/91) told the story of Beth Anne DeCiantis's attempt to qualify for the 1992 Olympic Trials marathon. A female runner must complete the 26-mile, 385-yard race in less than two hours, forty-five minutes to compete at the Olympic Trials.

Beth started strong but began having trouble around mile 23. She reached the final straightaway at 2:43, with just two minutes left to qualify. Two hundred yards from the finish, she stumbled and fell. Dazed, she stayed down for twenty seconds. The crowd yelled, "Get up!" The clock was ticking—2:44, less than a minute to go.

Beth Anne staggered to her feet and began walking. Five yards short of the finish, with ten seconds to go, she fell again. She began to crawl, the crowd cheering her on, and crossed the finish line on her hands and knees. Her time? Two hours, 44 minutes, 57 seconds.

Hebrews 12:1 reminds us to run our race with perseverance and never give up.

—Terry Fisher
(Courage, Faithfulness)

Dates used:_____

Gary Thomas writes in *Christianity Today:*
Thinking about eternity helps us retrieve [perspective]. I'm reminded of this every year when I figure my taxes. During the year, I rejoice at the paychecks and extra income, and sometimes I flinch when I write out the tithe and offering. I do my best to be a joyful giver, but I confess it is not always easy, especially when there are other perceived needs and wants.

At the end of the year, however, all of that changes. As I'm figuring my tax liability, I wince at every source of income and rejoice with every tithe and offering check—more income means more tax, but every offering and tithe means less tax. Everything is turned upside down, or perhaps, more appropriately, right-side up.

I suspect Judgment Day will be like that.

(Judgment Day, Stewardship)

Dates used:_____

Power

First, huge shovels dig house-sized scoops of lignite coal. Pulverized and loaded onto railroad boxcars, the coal travels to a generating plant in east Texas, where it is further crushed into powder. Superheated, this powder ignites like gasoline when blown into the huge furnaces that crank three turbines.

Whirring at 3,600 revolutions per minute, these turbines are housed in concrete-and-steel casings 100 feet long, 10 feet tall, and 10 feet across. They generate enough electricity for entire cities.

A visitor to this plant once asked the chief engineer, "Where do you store the electricity?"

"We don't store it," the engineer replied. "We just make it."

When a light switch is flipped on in Dallas one hundred miles west, it literally places a demand on the system; it registers at the generating plant and prompts greater output.

God's grace and power likewise cannot be stored. Though inexhaustible, they come in the measure required, at the moment of need.

—Reggie McNeal
(God's Power, Intercession)

Dates used:_____

Major Osipovich, an air force pilot for the former USSR, planned to give a talk at his children's school about peace. He would need time off during the day to give his talk, so he volunteered for night duty. That's how Major Osipovich found himself patrolling the skies over the eastern regions of the Soviet Union on September 1, 1983—the night Korean Air Lines Flight KE007 strayed into Soviet air space.

Soon the Soviet pilot was caught in a series of blunders and misinformation. In the end, Major Osipovich followed orders and shot down the unidentified aircraft. The actions of an air force major preparing to talk about peace plunged 240 passengers to their deaths and sparked an international incident that pushed world powers to a stand-off.

Our talk is important. But our actions carry far more weight.

(Actions, Consequences)

Dates used:_____

D ana Keeton told this story in *The Democratic Union* of Lawrenceburg, Tennessee:

The sun had just risen on a hot August day in 1944 in the small village of Plelo, in German–occupied France. The 15-year-old boy did not know why he and the other citizens of Plelo had been lined up before a firing squad in the middle of the town square. Perhaps they were being punished for harboring a unit of Marquisards, the French underground freedom fighters. Perhaps they were merely to satisfy the blood lust of the German commanding officer who, the evening before, had routed the small group of Marquisard scouts. All the boy knew was that he was about to die.

As he stood before the firing squad, he remembered the carefree days of his early childhood, before the war, spent roaming the green of the French countryside. He thought about all he would miss by never growing up. Most of all he was terrified of dying. *How will the bullets feel ripping through my body?* he wondered. He hoped no one could hear the whimperings coming from deep in his throat every time he exhaled.

Suddenly, the boy heard the sound of exploding mortar shells beyond the limits of his little village. The Germans were forced to abandon the firing squad and face a small unit of U.S. tanks with twenty GI's led by Bob Hamsley, a corporal in Patton's Third Army. A Marquisard captain had asked Hamsley for help. After three hours, fifty Nazis were dead, and the other fifty were taken prisoner.

In 1990, the town of Plelo honored Bob Hamsley on the very spot where dozens of the town's citizens would have died if not for him. The man who initiated the search for Hamsley and the ceremony honoring him was the former mayor of Plelo, that same 15-year-old boy. He had determined to find the man who saved his life and honor him.

It's hard to forget your savior.

—Tim Stafford
(Freedom, Salvation)

Dates used:_____

J ean Giono tells the story of Elzeard Bouffier, a
shepherd he met in 1913 in the French Alps.

At that time, because of careless deforestation,
the mountains around Provence, France, were barren.
Former villages were deserted because their springs
and brooks had run dry. The wind blew furiously,
unimpeded by foliage.

While mountain climbing, Giono came to a shepherd's hut, where he was invited to spend the night.

After dinner Giono watched the shepherd meticu-
lously sort through a pile of acorns, discarding those
that were cracked or undersized. When the shepherd
had counted out 100 perfect acorns, he stopped for
the night and went to bed.

Giono learned that the 55-year-old shepherd had
been planting trees on the wild hillsides for over
three years. He had planted 100,000 trees, 20,000 of
which had sprouted. Of those, he expected half to be
eaten by rodents or die due to the elements, and the
other half to live.

After World War I, Giono returned to the moun-
tainside and discovered incredible rehabilitation:
there was a veritable forest, accompanied by a chain
reaction in nature. Water flowed in the once-empty
brooks. The ecology, sheltered by a leafy roof and
bonded to the earth by a mat of spreading roots,
became hospitable. Willows, rushes, meadows,
gardens, and flowers were birthed.

Giono returned again after World War II. Twenty
miles from the lines, the shepherd had continued his
work, ignoring the war of 1939 just as he had

ignored that of 1914. The reformation of the land continued. Whole regions glowed with health and prosperity.

Giono writes: "On the site of the ruins I had seen in 1913 now stand neat farms. . . . The old streams, fed by the rains and snows that the forest conserves, are flowing again. . . . Little by little, the villages have been rebuilt. People from the plains, where land is costly, have settled here, bringing youth, motion, the spirit of adventure."

Those who pray are like spiritual reforesters, digging holes in barren land and planting the seeds of life. Through these seeds, dry spiritual wastelands are transformed into harvestable fields, and life-giving water is brought to parched and barren souls.

—Hal Seed
(Healing, Hope)

Dates used:_____

Prayer

According to the Associated Press, in September 1994 Cindy Hartman of Conway, Arkansas, walked into her house to answer the phone and was confronted by a burglar. He ripped the phone cord out of the wall and ordered her into a closet.

Hartman dropped to her knees and asked the burglar if she could pray for him. "I want you to know that God loves you and I forgive you," she said.

The burglar apologized for what he had done. Then he yelled out the door to a woman in a pickup truck: "We've got to unload all of this. This is a Christian home and a Christian family. We can't do this to them."

As Hartman remained on her knees, the burglar returned furniture he had taken from her home. Then he took the bullets out of his gun, handed the gun to Hartman, and walked out the door.

Praying for our enemies is incredibly disarming.

—Scott Harrison
(Courage, Intercession)

Dates used:_____

In *Point Man,* Steve Farrar tells the story of George McCluskey:

When McCluskey married and started a family, he decided to invest one hour a day in prayer, because he wanted his kids to follow Christ. After a time, he expanded his prayers to include his grandchildren and great-grandchildren. Every day between 11 A.M. and noon, he prayed for the next three generations.

As the years went by, his two daughters committed their lives to Christ and married men who went into full-time ministry. The two couples produced four girls and one boy. Each of the girls married a minister, and the boy became a pastor.

The first two children born to this generation were both boys. Upon graduation from high school, the two cousins chose the same college and became roommates. During their sophomore year, one boy decided to go into the ministry. The other didn't. He undoubtedly felt some pressure to continue the family legacy, but he chose instead to pursue his interest in psychology.

He earned his doctorate and eventually wrote books for parents that became bestsellers. He started a radio program heard on more than a thousand stations each day. The man's name—James Dobson.

Through his prayers, George McCluskey affected far more than one family.

—Loyal J. Martin
(Fathers, Persistency)

Dates used:_____

Presumption

The Associated Press ran the story of Andre-Francois Raffray. Thirty years ago, at the age of 47, he worked out a real estate deal with Jeanne Calment, then age 90. He would pay her $500 each month until her death, in order to secure ownership of her apartment in Arles, France. This is a common practice in France, benefiting both buyers and seniors on a fixed income.

Unfortunately for Raffray, Jeanne Calment has become the world's oldest living person. Still alive at 122, she outlived Raffray, who died in December 1995, at the age of 77. He paid $184,000 for an apartment he never lived in. According to the contract, Raffray's survivors must continue payment until Mrs. Calment dies.

James 4:13, 15 warns us of presuming to know what the future holds: "Now listen, you who say, 'Today or tomorrow we will go to this or that city, spend a year there, carry on business and make money. . . .' Instead, you ought to say, 'If it is the Lord's will, we will live and do this or that.' "

—Steve Abbott
(Aging, Uncertainty)

Dates used:_____

Homiletics (Jan.–Mar./96) told of a turtle who wanted to spend the winter in Florida, but he knew he could never walk that far. He convinced a couple of geese to help him, each taking one end of a piece of rope, while he clamped his vise-like jaws in the center.

The flight went fine until someone on the ground looked up in admiration and asked, "Who in the world thought of that?"

Unable to resist the chance to take credit, the turtle opened his mouth to shout, "I did—"

(Bragging, Cooperation)

Dates used:_____

Priorities

In 1992 Kerrin-Lee Gartner of Calgary, Alberta, became the first Canadian in history to win Olympic gold in the women's downhill. In Canada she was an immediate sensation.

Shortly after her victory, an announcer interviewing her commented that this must surely be the most significant day of her life.

"No," she replied. "The most significant day was the day of my marriage—but this ranks pretty high."

Even great achievements cannot compare with great relationships.

—Gerald Cameron
(Achievement, Marriage)

Dates used:_____

The only survivor of a shipwreck washed up on a small uninhabited island. He cried out to God to save him, and every day he scanned the horizon for help, but none seemed forthcoming.

Exhausted, he eventually managed to build a rough hut and put his few possessions in it. But then one day, after hunting for food, he arrived home to find his little hut in flames, the smoke rolling up to the sky. The worst had happened; he was stung with grief.

Early the next day, though, a ship drew near the island and rescued him.

"How did you know I was here?" he asked the crew.

"We saw your smoke signal," they replied.

Though it may not seem so now, your present difficulty may be instrumental to your future happiness.

—John Yates
(Difficulties, God's Sovereignty)

Dates used:_____

Racial Reconciliation

In 1963, George C. Wallace, governor of Alabama, literally stood in the door of the University of Alabama, preventing Vivian Malone Jones, a young African-American woman, from enrolling as a student. Thirty-three years later, Wallace awarded Jones the first Lurleen B. Wallace Award of Courage. (The award, named in honor of Wallace's wife, recognizes women who have made outstanding contributions to the state of Alabama.) Wallace publicly apologized to Jones for the 1963 controversy; Jones in turn forgave Wallace.

Robert F. Kennedy, Jr., on hand for the event, said, "This event really is a moment of reconciliation and redemption."

—Edward J. Robinson
(Forgiveness, Restitution)

Dates used:_____

A gem dealer was strolling the aisles at the Tucson Gem and Mineral Show when he noticed a blue-violet stone the size and shape of a potato. He looked it over, then as calmly as possible, asked the vendor, "You want $15 for *this?*" The seller, realizing the rock wasn't as pretty as others in the bin, lowered the price to $10.

The stone has since been certified as a 1,905-carat natural star sapphire, about 800 carats larger than the largest stone of its kind. It was appraised at $2.28 million.

It took a lover of stones to recognize the sapphire's worth. It took the Lover of Souls to recognize the true value of ordinary-looking people like us.

—Wanda Vassallo
(Value, Wealth)

Dates used:_____

Rejoicing

On a balmy October afternoon in 1982, Badger Stadium in Madison, Wisconsin, was packed. More than 60,000 die-hard University of Wisconsin supporters were watching their football team take on the Michigan State Spartans.

MSU had the better team. What seemed odd, however, as the score became more lopsided, were the bursts of applause and shouts of joy from the Wisconsin fans. How could they cheer when their team was losing?

It turned out that seventy miles away the Milwaukee Brewers were beating the St. Louis Cardinals in game three of the 1982 World Series. Many of the fans in the stands were listening to portable radios—and responding to something other than their immediate circumstances.

Paul encourages us to fix our eyes not on what is seen but what is unseen (2 Cor. 4:18). When we do, we can rejoice even in hardships because we see Christ's larger victory.

—Greg Asimakoupoulos
(Perspective, Victory)

Dates used:_____

In March 1995, The New England Pipe Cleaning Company of Watertown, Connecticut, was digging twenty-five feet beneath the streets of Revere, Massachusetts, in order to clean a clogged 10-inch sewer line.

In addition to the usual materials one might expect to find in a clogged sewer line, the three-man team found 61 rings, vintage coins, eyeglasses, and silverware, all of which they were allowed to keep.

Whether it's pipes or people, if you put up with some mess, sometimes you find real treasure.

—Stanley Carvell
(Hardship, Treasure)

Dates used:_____

Respect

In his book with Ken Blanchard, *Everyone's a Coach,* Don Shula tells of losing his temper near an open microphone during a televised game with the Los Angeles Rams. Millions of viewers were surprised and shocked by Shula's explicit profanity. Letters soon arrived from all over the country, voicing the disappointment of many who had respected the coach for his integrity.

Shula could have given excuses, but he didn't. Everyone who included a return address received a personal apology. He closed each letter by stating, "I value your respect and will do my best to earn it again."

There are two ways to gain respect. One is to act nobly. The other is, when you fail to do so, make no excuses.

(Apologizing, Excuses)

Dates used:_____

J udy Anderson grew up as the daughter of missionaries in Zaire. As a little girl, she went to a day-long rally celebrating the one-hundredth anniversary of Christian missionaries coming to that part of Zaire.

After a full day of long speeches and music, an old man came before the crowd and insisted that he be allowed to speak. He said he soon would die, and that he alone had some important information. If he did not speak, that information would go with him to his grave.

He explained that when Christian missionaries came a hundred years before, his people thought the missionaries were strange and their message unusual. The tribal leaders decided to test the missionaries by slowly poisoning them to death. Over a period of months and years, missionary children died one by one. Then the old man said, "It was as we watched how they died that we decided we wanted to live as Christians."

That story had gone untold for one hundred years. Those who died painful, strange deaths never knew why they were dying or what the impact of their lives and deaths would be. They stayed because they trusted Jesus Christ.

—Leith Anderson
(Courage, Trust)

Dates used:_____

Sacrifice

In *From Jerusalem to Irian Jaya,* Ruth Tucker writes about Dr. Eleanor Chestnut. After arriving in China in 1893 under the American Presbyterian missions board, Dr. Chestnut built a hospital, using her own money to buy bricks and mortar. The need for her services was so great, she performed surgery in her bathroom until the building was completed.

One operation involved the amputation of a common laborer's leg. Complications arose, and skin grafts were needed. A few days later, another doctor asked Chestnut why she was limping. "Oh, it's nothing," was her terse reply.

Finally, a nurse revealed that the skin graft for the patient, a coolie, came from Dr. Chestnut's own leg, taken with only local anesthetic.

During the Boxer Rebellion of 1905, Dr. Chestnut and four other missionaries were killed by a mob that stormed the hospital.

(Devotion, Martyrdom)

Dates used:_____

In *Executive Edge,* management-consultant Ken Blanchard retells the story of a little girl named Schia, which first appeared in *Chicken Soup for the Soul.* When Schia was 4 years old, her baby brother was born.

"Little Schia began to ask her parents to leave her alone with the new baby. They worried that, like most 4-year-olds, she might want to hit or shake him, so they said no."

Over time, though, since Schia wasn't showing signs of jealousy, they changed their minds and decided to let Schia have her private conference with the baby. "Elated, Schia went into the baby's room and shut the door, but it opened a crack—enough for her curious parents to peek in and listen. They saw little Schia walk quietly up to her baby brother, put her face close to his, and say, 'Baby, tell me what God feels like. I'm starting to forget.' "

Jesus taught that to enter the kingdom of God, we must receive it like a little child (Mark 10:15).

(Innocence, Wonder)

Dates used:_____

Sanctity of Life

Susan Shelley writes in *Marriage Partnership:*
In the fifth month of my pregnancy, our doctor recommended a Level II ultrasound. As I lay on the examining table, Dr. Silver manipulated the ultrasound, measuring the cranium and the femur and viewing the internal organs. We all watched the embryonic motions.

"Is everything okay?" Marshall asked. . . .

Moments later, Dr. Silver announced his observations in a matter-of-fact voice. "We have some problems. The fetus has a malformed heart—the aorta is attached incorrectly. There are missing portions of the cerebellum. A club foot. A cleft palate and perhaps a cleft lip. Possibly spina bifida. This is probably a case of Trisomy 13 or Trisomy 18. In either case, it is a condition incompatible with life."

Neither Marshall nor I could say anything. So Dr. Silver continued.

"It's likely the fetus will spontaneously miscarry. If the child is born, it will not survive long outside the womb. You need to decide if you want to try and carry this pregnancy to term."

We both knew what he was asking. My soul was shaken by the news, but I knew clearly what I was to do.

"God is the giver and taker of life," I said. "If the only opportunity I have to know this child is in my womb, I don't want to cut that time short. If the only world he is to know is the womb, I want that world to be as safe as I can make it."

(Courage, Motherhood)

Dates used:_____

The Winter 1991 issue of the *University of Pacific Review* offers a chilling description of the 1986 Chernobyl nuclear disaster:

There were two electrical engineers in the control room that night, and the best thing that could be said for what they were doing is they were "playing around" with the machine. They were performing what the Soviets later described as an unauthorized experiment. They were trying to see how long a turbine would "free wheel" when they took the power off it.

Now, taking the power off that kind of a nuclear reactor is a difficult, dangerous thing to do, because these reactors are very unstable in their lower ranges. In order to get the reactor down to that kind of power, where they could perform the test they were interested in performing, they had to override manually six separate computer-driven alarm systems. One by one the computers would come up and say, "Stop! Dangerous! Go no further!" And one by one, rather than shutting off the experiment, they shut off the alarms and kept going. You know the results: nuclear fallout that was recorded all around the world, from the largest industrial accident ever to occur in the world.

The instructions and warnings in Scripture are just as clear. We ignore them at our own peril, and tragically, at the peril of innocent others.

—Tom Tripp
(Consequences, Recklessness)

Dates used:_____

Second Coming

Ray Bakke shares this story:

I knew an old Glasgow professor named Mac-Donald who, along with a Scottish chaplain, was put in a prison camp. A high wire fence separated the Americans from the British. MacDonald was put in the American barracks, the chaplain with the Brits.

Unknown to the guards, the Americans had a little homemade radio and were able to get news from the outside. Everyday, MacDonald would take a headline or two to the fence and share it with the chaplain in the ancient Gaelic language, indecipherable to the Germans.

One day, news came over the little radio that the German high command had surrendered and the war was over. MacDonald took the news to his friend, then watched him disappear into the barracks. A moment later, a roar of celebration came from the barracks.

Life in that camp was transformed. Men walked around singing and shouting, waving at the guards, even laughing at the dogs. When the German guards finally heard the news three nights later, they fled into the dark, leaving the gates unlocked. The next morning, Brits and Americans walked out as free men. Yet they had truly been set free three days earlier by the news that the war was over.

While Christ's Kingdom is not fully achieved, we know the outcome of the battle. We too have been set free.

(Good News, Hope)

Dates used:_____

W hen Harry Truman was thrust into the presidency, by the death of Franklin Delano Roosevelt, Sam Rayburn took him aside.

"From here on out, you're going to have lots of people around you. They'll try to put up a wall around you and cut you off from any ideas but theirs. They'll tell you what a great man you are, Harry. But you and I both know you ain't."

(Candor, Wisdom)

Dates used:_____

E xecutive consultant Richard Hagberg told this story:

The head of one large company recently told me about an incident that occurred as he and his wife waited in line to get his driver's license renewed. He was frustrated at how long it was taking and grumbled to his wife, "Don't they know who I am?"

She replied, "Yeah, you're a plumber's son who got lucky."

—*Fortune* (6/26/96)
(Impatience, Pride)

Dates used:_____

Selflessness

In *The Trivialization of God,* Donald McCullough quotes Freeman Patterson, noted Canadian photographer, describing barriers that prevented him from seeing the best photo possibilities:

Letting go of the self is an essential precondition to real seeing. When you let go of yourself, you abandon any preconceptions about the subject matter which might cramp you into photographing in a certain, predetermined way. . . .

When you let go, new conceptions arise from your direct experience of the subject matter, and new ideas and feelings will guide you as you make pictures.

In the spiritual life, just as in photography, being preoccupied with self is the greatest barrier to seeing. But when we get past it, we catch glimpses of extraordinary beauty.

—Merle Mees
(Perspective, Selfishness)

Dates used:_____

Perhaps no composer has captured the musical heart and soul of America as did Irving Berlin. In addition to familiar favorites such as "God Bless America" and "Easter Parade," he wrote, "I'm Dreaming of a White Christmas," which still ranks as the all-time bestselling musical score.

In an interview for the *San Diego Union,* Don Freeman asked Berlin, "Is there any question you've never been asked that you would like someone to ask you?"

"Well, yes, there is one," he replied. " 'What do you think of the many songs you've written that didn't become hits?' My reply would be that I still think they are wonderful."

God, too, has an unshakable delight in what—and whom—he has made. He thinks each of his children is wonderful. Whether they're a "hit" in the eyes of others or not, he will always think they're wonderful.

—Jim Adams
(Creation, God's Love)

Dates used:_____

Self-worth

Charles Colson and several other Christian leaders once met with President Borja of Ecuador to discuss Prison Fellowship International's ministry in Ecuadorian penitentiaries. They had no sooner been seated in luxurious leather chairs when the President interrupted the conversation with the story of his own imprisonment years before being elected to the presidency.

He had been involved in the struggle for democracy in Ecuador. The military cracked down, and he was arrested. Without trial, they threw him into a cold dungeon with no light and no window. For three days he endured the solitary fear and darkness that can drive a person mad.

Just when the situation seemed unbearable, the huge steel door opened, and someone crept into the darkness. Borja heard the person working on something in the opposite corner. Then the figure crept out, closed the door, and disappeared.

Minutes later the room suddenly blazed with light. Someone, perhaps taking his life into his hands, had connected electricity to the broken light fixture. "From that moment," explained President Borja, "my imprisonment had meaning because at least I could see."

Even more important than the light we see with our eyes is the light that Christ brings to our hearts, giving our lives the understanding and meaning only he can give.

—Ronald W. Nikkel
(Light, Understanding)

Dates used:_____

T*he Los Angeles Times* (12/15/96) reported that David Suna and John Tu sold 80 percent of their company, Kingston Technology Corp., the world's largest manufacturer of computer memory products, for $1.5 billion dollars.

The two men decided to share their windfall with their employees. The average bonus payment their workers received was just over $75,000. Suna summarized their decision: "To share our success with everybody is the most joy we can have."

—Scot Snyder
(Joy, Success)

Dates used:_____

Significance

Frank Capra, who directed *It's a Wonderful Life*, was asked years ago about the central message of his classic film. After thinking a few moments, Capra responded, "I believe the real message of *It's a Wonderful Life* is this: that under the sun, nothing is insignificant to God." Now, when you watch the movie again, you know that everything that happens has intended and unintended consequences. Everything, because it happened, causes something else to happen. Everybody in that story is important, because he or she relates to everyone else. Nothing is insignificant under the sun to God.

Perhaps you need to be reminded, not only that you are important to God, but also that everyone around you is significant to him, too.

—Jay Akkerman
(God's Love, Hope)

Dates used:_____

In his book *Fuzzy Memories*, Jack Handey writes:
There used to be this bully who would demand
my lunch money every day. Since I was smaller, I
would give it to him. Then I decided to fight back.
I started taking karate lessons. But then the karate
lesson guy said I had to start paying him five dollars
a lesson. So I just went back to paying the bully.

*Too many people feel it is easier just to pay the
bully than it is to learn how to defeat him.*

—Sherman L. Burford
(Capitulation, Self-defense)

Dates used:_____

For eight years Sally had been the Romero family
pet. When they got her, she was only one foot
long. But Sally grew until eventually she reached
eleven-and-a-half feet and weighed eighty pounds.

On July 20, 1993, Sally, a Burmese python,
turned on 15-year-old Derek, strangling the teenager
until he died of suffocation. Associated Press Online
(7/22/93) quoted the police as saying that the snake
was "quite aggressive, hissing, and reacting" when
they arrived to investigate.

*Sins that seem little and harmless will grow.
Tolerate or ignore sin, and it will eventually lead
to death (James 1:15).*

—Bruce E. Truman
(Consequences, Death)

Dates used:_____

Sin

In 1991, a judge fined brothers Geno and Russell Capozziello, owners of a Bridgeport, Connecticut, wrecking company, nearly $900,000 for operating an illegal dump. In 1986, on the empty lots surrounding their facility, the brothers began dumping debris from buildings. Eventually the mound of rubble and muck covered two acres and reached a height of thirty-five feet, the equivalent of a three-story building.

The state ordered them to clean it up, but the brothers claimed there was no place to dump it legally in Bridgeport, and they could not afford to have it hauled away. While spending more than $330,000 the previous year to have debris hauled away, they barely dented the pile. According to Geno, "It was never supposed to get this high."

Like garbage, the effects of sinful habits have a way of accumulating beyond our plans and beyond our control.

—Michael E. Hardin
(Accumulation, Consequences of Sin)

Dates used:_____

Scores of people lost their lives. The world's mightiest army was forced to abandon a strategic base. Property damage approached a billion dollars. All because the sleeping giant, Mount Pinatube in the Philippines, roared back to life after six hundred years of quiet slumber.

When asked to account for the incredible destruction caused by this volcano, a research scientist from the Philippines Department of Volcanology observed, "When a volcano is silent for many years, our people forget that it's a volcano and begin to treat it like a mountain."

Like Mount Pinatube, our sinful nature always has the potential to erupt, bringing great harm both to ourselves and to others. The biggest mistake we can make is to ignore the volcano and move back onto what seems like a dormant "mountain."

—Stephen Schertzinger
(Destruction, Watchfulness)

Dates used:_____

Sinful Nature

The famous cuckoo bird never builds its own nest. It flies around until it sees another nest with eggs in it and no mother bird around. The cuckoo quickly lands, lays its eggs there, and flies away.

The thrush, whose nest has been invaded, comes back. Not being very good at arithmetic, she gets to work hatching the eggs. What happens? Four little thrushes hatch, but one large cuckoo hatches. The cuckoo is two or three times the size of the thrushes.

When Mrs. Thrush brings to the nest one large, juicy worm, she finds four petite thrush mouths, one cavernous cuckoo mouth. Guess who gets the worm? A full-sized thrush ends up feeding a baby cuckoo that is three times as big as it is.

Over time, the bigger cuckoo gets bigger and bigger, and the little thrushes get smaller and smaller. You can always find a baby cuckoo's nest. You walk along a hedgerow until you find dead little thrushes, which the cuckoo throws out one at a time.

Paul teaches in Romans 8:5–8 that spiritually speaking, you've got two natures in one nest. The nature that you go on feeding will grow, and the nature that you go on starving will diminish.

—Stuart Briscoe
(New Birth, Spiritual Growth)

Dates used:_____

I n *The Encourager,* Charles Mylander writes:
Los Angeles motorcycle police officer Bob Vernon saw a red pickup truck speed through a stop sign. *This guy must be late to work,* he thought to himself. He turned on his emergency lights and radioed that he was in pursuit. The pickup pulled over, and the officer approached.

Meanwhile, the driver thought, *The cops already know!* He rested his hand on the same gun he had used a few moments before to rob a twenty-four-hour market. The sack of stolen money was beside him.

The officer said, "May I see your—"

He never finished the sentence. The driver shoved his gun toward the policeman's chest and fired. The cop was knocked flat seven feet away.

A few seconds later, to the shock of the criminal, the officer stood up, pulled his service revolver, and fired twice. The first bullet went through the open window and smashed the windshield. The second tore through the door and ripped into the driver's left leg.

"Don't shoot!" the thief screamed, throwing the gun and sack of money out the pickup window.

What saved the policeman's life was Kevlar™, the super strong fabric used for bulletproof vests. Only three-eighths of an inch thick, Kevlar can stop bullets cold.

In Ephesians 6, the Bible instructs every Christian to put on the full armor of God.

—Mike Neifert
(Righteousness, Satan's Attack)

Dates used:_____

Spiritual Discipline

In the movie *Karate Kid,* young Daniel asks Mister Miagi to teach him karate. Miagi agrees under one condition: Daniel must submit totally to his instruction and never question his methods.

Daniel shows up the next day eager to learn. To his chagrin, Miagi has him paint a fence. Miagi demonstrates the precise motion for the job: up and down, up and down. Next, Miagi has him scrub the deck using a prescribed stroke. Daniel wonders, *What does this have to do with karate?* but says nothing.

Next, Miagi tells Daniel to wash and wax three weather-beaten cars and again prescribes the motion. Finally, Daniel reaches his limit: "I thought you were going to teach me karate, but all you have done is have me do your unwanted chores!"

Daniel has broken Miagi's one condition, and the old man's face pulses with anger. "I have been teaching you karate! Defend yourself!"

Miagi thrusts his arm at Daniel, who instinctively defends himself with an arm motion exactly like that used in one of his chores. Miagi unleashes a vicious kick, and again Daniel averts the blow with a motion used in his chores. After Daniel successfully defends himself from several more blows, Miagi simply walks away, leaving Daniel to discover what the master had known all along: skill comes from repeating the correct but seemingly mundane actions.

The same is true of godliness.

—Duke Winser
(Repetition, Submission)

Dates used:_____

In 1986 two brothers who live in a kibbutz near the Sea of Galilee made an incredible discovery. As these two Israeli fishermen monitored their equipment on the beaches of Gennesaret, they noticed something they'd not seen before. Something covered with mud glistened in the sun. Upon examination, archeologists determined that what the brothers had discovered was a fishing boat dating from the time of Jesus.

The only reason the artifact was discovered was because of a three-year drought, resulting in unusually low water in the lake.

The Bible tells us that in times of spiritual dryness, God may uncover something of fabulous value within—his presence (2 Cor. 4:7ff.).

—Greg Asimakoupoulos
(*Archaeology, God's Presence*)

Dates used:_____

He wanted to conduct. His conducting style, however, was idiosyncratic. During soft passages he'd crouch extremely low. For loud sections, he'd often leap into the air, even shouting to the orchestra.

His memory was poor. Once he forgot that he had instructed the orchestra not to repeat a section of music. During the performance, when he went back to repeat that section, they went forward, so he stopped the piece, hollering, "Stop! Wrong! That will not do! Again! Again!"

For his own piano concerto, he tried conducting from the piano. At one point he jumped from the bench, bumping the candles off the piano. At another concert he knocked over a choir boy.

During one long, delicate passage, he jumped high to cue a loud entrance, but nothing happened because he had lost count and signaled the orchestra too soon.

As his hearing worsened, musicians tried to ignore his conducting and get their cues from the first violinist.

Finally the musicians pled with him to go home and give up conducting, which he did.

He was Ludwig van Beethoven.

As the man whom many consider to be the greatest composer of all time learned, no one is a genius of all trades.

—David Sacks
(Example, Leadership)

Dates used:_____

Aqaba in 1917 seemed inpregnable. Any enemy vessel approaching the port would have to face the battery of huge naval guns above the town. Behind Aqaba in every direction lay barren, waterless, inhospitable desert. To the east lay the deadly "anvil of the sun." The Turks believed Aqaba to be safe from any attack. But they were wrong.

Lawrence of Arabia led a force of irregular Arab cavalry across the "anvil of the sun." Together, they rallied support among the local people. On July 6, 1917, the Arab forces swept into Aqaba from the north, from the blind side. A climactic moment of the magnificent film *Lawrence of Arabia* is the long, panning shot of the Arabs on their camels and horses, with Lawrence at their head, galloping past the gigantic naval guns that are completely powerless to stop them. The guns were facing in the wrong direction. Aqaba fell, and the Turkish hold on Palestine was broken, to be replaced by the British mandate and eventually by the State of Israel.

The Turks failed to defend Aqaba because they made two mistakes. They did not know their enemy, and they did not have the right weapons.

We must be careful not to make the same mistakes. Ephesians 6:12 makes it very clear who our enemy is: "Our struggle is not against flesh and blood, but against the rulers, against the authorities, against the powers of this dark world."

—Michael Boyland
(*Spiritual Armor, Wisdom*)

Dates used:_____

Spiritual Warfare

During Operation Desert Storm, the Iraqi war machine was overwhelmed by the Coalition Forces' ability to strike strategic targets with never-seen-before accuracy. Unknown to the Iraqis, the Allied Supreme Command had dropped Special Operations Forces (SOF) deep behind enemy lines. These men provided bombing coordinates for military targets and first-hand reports on the effectiveness of subsequent bombing missions.

To avoid unintended targets, pinpoint bombing was often required. A soldier from a SOF unit standing on the ground would request an aircraft high overhead to drop a laser-guided missile. Using a hand-held laser, the soldier would point at the target. The missile would hone in on the soldier's target for the hit.

In much the same way, the prayers of Christians focus the attention of the spiritual powers on high.

—Steve Schertzinger
(Intercession, Prayer)

Dates used:_____

Oseola McCarty, 87, did one thing all her life: laundry. Now she's famous for it—or at least for what she did with her profits.

For decades, Miss McCarty earned 50 cents per load doing laundry for the well-to-do families of Hattiesburg, Mississippi, preferring a washboard over an electric washing machine. Every week, she put a little bit in a savings account. When she finally retired, she asked her banker how much money she had socked away.

"$250,000," was his reply. She was in shock. "I had more than I could use in the bank," she explained. "I can't carry anything away from here with me, so I thought it was best to give it to some child to get an education."

This shy, never-married laundry woman gave $150,000 to nearby University of Southern Mississippi to help African-American young people attend college. "It's more blessed to give than to receive," she tells reporters. "I've tried it."

—Christian Reader
(*Frugality, Generosity*)

Dates used:_____

Strength

R ichard Mylander shares the following story:
On my way to a conference in Colorado, I was driving uphill along a major interstate when I overtook a freight train going the same direction at a slower speed. The train was being pushed uphill by two locomotives that sounded as if they were straining at full power. I'm a flatlander from the Midwest. *Is this how trains move in mountainous terrain?* I wondered.

A few minutes later, I gradually came alongside the front of the nearly mile-long string of cars. There I found five more locomotives pulling the train. Seven engines in all! Where I come from, I rarely see more than three.

That train was a lesson for me. I had been under serious strain for some time. I was feeling tired and was wondering whether I could persevere under the pressure.

How like God, I thought. When I am pushing a load uphill with all the strength I have and feel like my energy level is depleted, he wants me to know that he is in the lead pulling with power far greater than mine.

(God's Power, Perseverance)

Dates used:_____

For two years, scientists sequestered themselves in an artificial environment called *Biosphere 2*. Inside their self-sustaining community, the Biospherians created a number of mini-environments, including a desert, rain forest, even an ocean. Nearly every weather condition could be simulated except one, wind.

Over time, the effects of their windless environment became apparent. A number of acacia trees bent over and even snapped. Without the stress of wind to strengthen the wood, the trunks grew weak and could not hold up their own weight.

Though our culture shuns hardship, we would do well to remember that God uses it "for our good, that we may share in his holiness" (Heb. 12:10).

—Jay Akkerman
(Hardship, Strength)

Dates used:_____

Stubbornness

Between two farms near Valleyview, Alberta, you can find two parallel fences, only two feet apart, running for a half mile. Why are there two fences when one would do?

Two farmers, Paul and Oscar, had a disagreement that erupted into a feud. Paul wanted to build a fence between their land and split the cost, but Oscar was unwilling to contribute. Since he wanted to keep cattle on his land, Paul went ahead and built the fence anyway.

After the fence was completed, Oscar said to Paul, "I see we have a fence."

"What do you mean 'we'?" Paul replied. "I got the property line surveyed and built the fence two feet into my land. That means some of my land is outside the fence. And if any of your cows sets foot on my land, I'll shoot it."

Oscar knew Paul wasn't joking, so when he eventually decided to use the land adjoining Paul's for pasture, he was forced to build another fence, two feet away.

Oscar and Paul are both gone now, but their double fence stands as a monument to the high price we pay for stubbornness.

—Daren Wride
(Conflict, Neighbors)

Dates used:_____

Chuck Colson writes:
   When I was at Buckingham Palace last year, Prince Philip asked me, "What can we do about crime here in England?"

I replied, "Send more children to Sunday school." He thought I was joking. But I pointed out a study by sociologist Christie Davies, which found that in the first half of the 1800s British society was marked by high levels of crime and violence, which dropped dramatically in the late 1800s and early 1900s. What changed an entire nation's national character? Throughout that period, attendance at Sunday schools rose steadily until, by 1888, a full 75 percent of children in England were enrolled. Since then, attendance has fallen off to one-third its peak level, with a corresponding increase in crime and disorder. If we fill the Sunday schools, we can change hearts and restore society.

—*Jubilee* (October 1995)
(Children, Crime)

Dates used:_____

Support

arl G. Conner shares this story:

A few winters ago, we had a number of extremely heavy snows in the Forsyth County area of North Carolina. Between Winston-Salem and Kernersville, along interstate I–40, were several large groves of tall, young pine trees.

Following one of the six-inch wet snows, the pine branches were bowed down with the weight of the heavy snow. The thick grove of trees looked like a picture out of a story book.

In addition to the groves of pines, a good many trees stood alone in the more sparsely wooded areas next to the interstate. Without the protection of being able to lean one against another, many of the beautiful trees broke off and fell to the ground. However, the trees that were in groves bent under the load of the snow, leaning one against another. In the thick groves, none of the pines were broken.

One was reminded of the importance of standing together in the time of storm. There is strength in leaning one against another.

(Interdependence, Teamwork)

Dates used:_____

In the summer of 1989, Mark Wellman, a paraplegic, gained national recognition by climbing the sheer granite face of El Capitan in Yosemite National Park. On the seventh and final day of his climb, the headlines of *The Fresno Bee* read, "Showing a Will of Granite." Accompanying the headline was a photo of Wellman being carried on the shoulders of his climbing companion Mike Corbett. A subtitle said, "Paraplegic and partner prove no wall is too high to scale."

What many people did not know is that Mike Corbett scaled the face of El Capitan three times in order to help Mark Wellman pull himself up once.

—Greg Asimakoupoulos
(Friendship, Teamwork)

Dates used:_____

Suspicion

The *San Francisco Examiner* (7/7/93) reported that the California State Automobile Association claims office received a package by Federal Express. The unknown contents were bundled in a Fruit Loops cereal box.

Workers quickly became suspicious. The FBI had only days before uncovered a terrorist bombing ring in New York, and the media had been crackling with stories of terrorist bombings.

Security guards called the police, and about 400 office workers were evacuated from the building. The bomb squad soon arrived on the scene. The Fruit Loops cereal box was "neutralized" with a small cannon, and its contents were blasted into the air. The bomb squad, however, found no explosives. Inside the suspicious package had been $24,000 in cash. The box contained bundles of $20 bills, $1,000 of which were destroyed in the blast.

"This was a first, finding money," said platoon leader Jim Seim. The package "arrived in such a way that it aroused our suspicions," he said. "We were able to render it neutral. We always err on the side of caution."

In our world it is prudent to use caution, but blanket suspicion can destroy things more valuable than money. Perhaps that is why Christ told us to be shrewd as snakes, and innocent as doves.

—Craig Brian Larson
(Caution, Innocence)

Dates used:_____

Herman Ostry's barn floor was under twenty-nine inches of water because of a rising creek. The Bruno, Nebraska, farmer invited a few friends to a barn raising. He needed to move his entire 17,000-pound barn to a new foundation more than 143 feet away. His son Mike devised a lattice work of steel tubing, and nailed, bolted, and welded it on the inside and the outside of the barn. Hundreds of handles were attached.

After one practice lift, 344 volunteers slowly walked the barn up a slight incline, each supporting less than fifty pounds. In just three minutes, the barn was on its new foundation.

The body of Christ can accomplish great things when we work together.

—Joseph F. Mlaker
(Accomplishments, Cooperation)

Dates used:_____

Thanksgiving

The Masai tribe in West Africa have an unusual way of saying thank-you. Translators tell us that when the Masai express thanks, they bow, put their foreheads on the ground, and say, "My head is in the dirt."

When members of another African tribe want to express gratitude, they sit for a long time in front of the hut of the person who did the favor and literally say, "I sit on the ground before you."

These Africans understand well what thanksgiving is and why it's difficult for us: at its core, thanksgiving is an act of humility.

—Joel Gregory
(Gratitude, Humility)

Dates used:_____

While on a short-term missions trip, Pastor Jack Hinton was leading worship at a leper colony on the island of Tobago. A woman who had been facing away from the pulpit turned around.

"It was the most hideous face I had ever seen," Hinton said. "The woman's nose and ears were entirely gone. She lifted a fingerless hand in the air and asked, 'Can we sing Count Your Many Blessings?' "

Overcome with emotion, Hinton left the service. He was followed by a team member who said, "I guess you'll never be able to sing that song again."

"Yes I will," he replied, "but I'll never sing it the same way."

—*The Pastor's Update* (5/96)
(Gratitude, Joy)

Dates used:_____

On September 11, 1995, a squirrel climbed on the Metro-North Railroad power lines near New York City. This set off an electrical surge, which weakened an overhead bracket, which let a wire dangle toward the tracks, which tangled in a train, which tore down all the lines. As a result, 47,000 commuters were stuck in Manhattan for hours that evening.

As James 3:5–6 teaches us, even something as small as the tongue can cause a lot of damage.

—Sherman L. Burford
(Consequences, Gossip)

Dates used:_____

Trust

In May 1995, Randy Reid, a 34-year-old construction worker, was welding on top of a nearly completed water tower outside Chicago. According to writer Melissa Ramsdell, Reid unhooked his safety gear to reach for some pipes when a metal cage slipped and bumped the scaffolding on which he stood. The scaffolding tipped, and Reid lost his balance. He fell 110 feet, landing face down on a pile of dirt, just missing rocks and construction debris.

A fellow worker called 911. When paramedics arrived, they found Reid conscious, moving, and complaining of a sore back.

Apparently the fall didn't cost Reid his sense of humor. As paramedics carried him on a backboard to the ambulance, Reid had one request: "Don't drop me." (Doctors later said Reid came away from the accident with just a bruised lung.)

Sometimes we resemble that construction worker. God protects us from harm in a 110-foot fall, but we're still nervous about three-foot heights. The God who saved us from hell and death can protect us from the smaller dangers we face this week.

—Greg Asimakoupoulos
(Protection, Worry)

Dates used:_____

The Department of Transportation has set aside $200 million dollars for research and testing of an Automated Highway System. This system would purportedly relieve traffic woes with "super cruise control" in heavily congested cities.

Special magnets imbedded in the asphalt every four feet would transfer signals between vehicle and main computer system. Steering, acceleration and braking would be controlled by sensors, computer navigation systems and cameras along the side of the road. Control would be returned to drivers at their specified exit.

Researchers and government officials claim they have the technological capability to address any potential problem. The one challenge they have yet to address?

Says Mike Doble, Buick's technology manager, "The only thing we can't do yet is get people to comfortably trust the system. It's not a technology issue. Would *you* drive, closely spaced, at high speeds, through San Diego?"

Trust is always the question. "Trust in the Lord with all your heart and lean not on your own understanding; in all your ways, acknowledge him, and he will make your paths straight" (Prov. 3:5–6).

—USA Today (4/9/97)
(Faith, Obedience)

Dates used:_____

Trust

Gladys Aylward, missionary to China more than fifty years ago, was forced to flee when the Japanese invaded Yangcheng. But she could not leave her work behind. With only one assistant, she led more than a hundred orphans over the mountains toward Free China.

In their book *The Hidden Price of Greatness,* Ray Besson and Ranelda Mack Hunsicker tell what happened:

During Gladys's harrowing journey out of war-torn Yangcheng . . . she grappled with despair as never before. After passing a sleepless night, she faced the morning with no hope of reaching safety.

A 13-year-old girl in the group reminded her of their much-loved story of Moses and the Israelites crossing the Red Sea.

"But I am not Moses," Gladys cried in desperation.

"Of course you aren't," the girl said, "but Jehovah is still God!"

When Gladys and the orphans made it through, they proved once again that no matter how inadequate we feel, God is still God, and we can trust in him.

—Jonathan G. Yandell
(God's Care, Inadequacy)

Dates used:_____

I n *The New Doublespeak: Why No One Knows What Anyone's Saying Anymore,* author William Lutz defines a few of the more creative doublespeak terms currently in vogue:

 • *Meaningful downturn in aggregate output* (recession)
  • *After-sales service* (kickback)
  • *Resource development park* (trash dump)
  • *Temporarily displaced inventory* (stolen goods)
  • *Strategic misrepresentation* (lie)
  • *Reality augmentation* (lie)
  • *Terminological inexactitude* (lie).

—*Copy Editor* (Oct/Nov 1996)
(Deceit, Lying)

Dates used:_____

Truth

In the classroom setting of one *Peanuts* comic strip, on the first day of the new school year, the students were told to write an essay about returning to class. In her essay Lucy wrote, "Vacations are nice, but it's good to get back to school. There is nothing more satisfying or challenging than education, and I look forward to a year of expanding knowledge."

Needless to say, the teacher was pleased with Lucy and complimented her fine essay. In the final frame, Lucy leans over and whispers to Charlie Brown, "After a while, you learn what sells."

The temptation to say "what sells," what others want to hear whether it is true or not, is always with us.

—William M. Nieporte
(Deceit, Guile)

Dates used:_____

Time (1/22/95) reported that the earthquake in Kobe, Japan, occurred when two plates on a fault line fifteen miles offshore suddenly shifted against each other, violently lurching six to ten feet in opposite directions. The result was the worst Japanese earthquake since 1923. Thousands died. More than 46,000 buildings lay in ruins. One-fifth of the city's population was left instantly homeless.

The destruction unleashed by those two tectonic plates depicts what happens when a Christian bonds unequally with a non-Christian. Two people committed to each other but going in different directions can lead only to trouble.

—David Farnum
(Marriage, Relationships)

Dates used:_____

Ungratefulness

A man writing at the post office desk was approached by an older fellow with a postcard in his hand. The old man said, "Sir, could you please address this postcard for me?"

The man gladly did so, then agreed to write a short message and sign the card for the man. Finally the younger man asked, "Is there anything else I can do for you?"

The old fellow thought about it for a moment and said, "Yes, at the end could you put, 'P.S. Please excuse the sloppy handwriting.' "

Why is it that we often complain against those who do the most for us?

—John Yates
(Complaining, Criticism)

Dates used:_____

Comedian Emo Philips used to tell this story:
In conversation with a person I had recently met, I asked, "Are you Protestant or Catholic?"

My new acquaintance replied, "Protestant."

I said, "Me too! What franchise?"

He answered, "Baptist."

"Me too!" I said. "Northern Baptist or Southern Baptist?"

"Northern Baptist," he replied.

"Me too!" I shouted.

We continued to go back and forth. Finally I asked, "Northern conservative fundamentalist Baptist, Great Lakes Region, Council of 1879 or Northern conservative fundamentalist Baptist, Great Lakes Region, Council of 1912?"

He replied, "Northern conservative fundamentalist Baptist, Great Lakes Region, Council of 1912."

I said, "Die, heretic!"

—New Republic
(Denominations, Dissension)

Dates used:_____

The Unknown

An Arab chief tells the story of a spy captured and sentenced to death by a general in the Persian army. This general had the strange custom of giving condemned criminals a choice between the firing squad and "the big, black door."

The moment for execution drew near, and guards brought the spy to the Persian general. "What will it be," asked the general, "the firing squad or 'the big, black door?' "

The spy hesitated for a long time. Finally he chose the firing squad.

A few minutes later, hearing the shots ring out confirming the spy's execution, the general turned to his aide and said, "They always prefer the known to the unknown. People fear what they don't know. Yet, we gave him a choice."

"What lies beyond the big door?" asked the aide.

"Freedom," replied the general. "I've known only a few brave enough to take that door."

The best opportunities in our lives stand behind the forbidding door of the great unknown.

—Don McCullough
(Courage, Freedom)

Dates used:_____

L yle Arakaki shares this insight:
In Hawaii, because of the time difference with the continental U.S., the NFL Monday Night Football game is played in mid-afternoon, so the local TV station delays its telecast until 6:30 in the evening.

When my favorite team plays, I'm too excited to wait for television, so I'll listen to the game on the radio, which broadcasts it live. Then, because they're my favorite team, I'll watch the game on television, too.

If I know my team has won the game, it influences how I watch it on television. If my team fumbles the ball or throws an interception, it's not a problem. I think, *That's bad, but it's okay. In the end, we'll win!*"

"In this world you will have trouble," said Jesus. "But take heart! I have overcome the world" (John 16:33).

When going through trouble, knowing the final outcome makes all the difference.

(Perspective, Trouble)

Dates used:_____

Vigilance

The January 13, 1992, issue of *Fortune* featured the "Biggest Business Goofs of 1991."

In an act of corporate cooperation, AT&T reached an agreement with the power company in New York City, ConEd. The contract stated that whenever power demands exceeded the utility's grid, AT&T would lessen their demands on the electric utility by throwing a switch, unplugging some of its facilities, and drawing power from internal generators at its 33 Thomas Street station in lower Manhattan.

On September 17, AT&T acted in accordance with its agreement. But when AT&T's own generators kicked in, the power surge kicked out some of their vital rectifiers, which handled 4.5 million domestic calls, 470,000 international calls, 1,174 flights across the nation carrying 85,000 passengers, and the total communications systems linking air traffic controllers at La Guardia, Kennedy, and Newark airports.

The alarm bells at the 33 Thomas Street station rang unheeded for six hours. The AT&T personnel in charge of the rectifiers were away attending a one-day seminar on how to handle emergencies.

—Phillip W. Gunter
(Emergencies, Preparation)

Dates used:_____

In *More than You and Me*, Kevin and Karen Miller write of the power of a God-given vision:

One couple lived in London 130 years ago. For the first 10 years of their marriage, William Booth, especially, was in a quandary: What was God calling him to do?

Then his wife, Catherine, a skillful Bible teacher, was invited to preach in London. While they were there, William took a late-night walk through the slums of London's East End. Every fifth building was a pub. Most had steps at the counter so little children could climb up and order gin. That night he told Catherine, "I seemed to hear a voice sounding in my ears, 'Where can you go and find such heathen as these, and where is there so great a need for your labors?' Darling, I have found my destiny!"

Later that year, 1865, the couple opened the "Christian Mission" in London's slums. Their life vision: to reach the "down and outers" that other Christians ignored. That simple vision of two people grew into the Salvation Army, which now ministers through three million members in ninety-one countries.

(Ministry, Mission)

Dates used:_____

Wants and Needs

In his book *Maverick,* Ricardo Semler tells of a lesson he learned working at Semco:

We were in yet another meeting . . . when we came to the purchase of $50,000 worth of file cabinets. Several departments had been waiting months for the cabinets and in desperation had decided to pool their requests. . . .

We didn't buy a single new file cabinet that day. Instead, we decided to stop the company for half a day and hold the First Biannual Semco File Inspection and Clean-out. . . .

Our instructions were simple: We told everyone to look inside every file folder and purge every nonessential piece of paper. . . .

I was one of Semco's biggest file hogs, with four large cabinets and a request for two more. After our cleanup, I trimmed down to a single cabinet, and that was pretty much how it went throughout the company. . . . The cleanup went so well that when everyone had finished, Semco auctioned off dozens of unneeded file cabinets.

Sometimes what we think we need isn't what we really need. When we pray, we learn to distinguish between needs and wants.

—Terry Fisher
(Excess, Greed)

Dates used:_____

The *Chicago Tribune* (9/1/96) ran the story of Buddy Post, "living proof that money can't buy happiness." In 1988, he won $16.2 million in the Pennsylvania Lottery. Since then, he was convicted "of assault, his sixth wife left him, his brother was convicted of trying to kill him, and his landlady successfully sued him for one-third of the jackpot.

"Money didn't change me," insists Post, a 58-year-old former carnival worker and cook. "It changed people around me that I knew, that I thought cared a little bit about me. But they only cared about the money."

Post is trying to auction off seventeen future payments, valued at nearly $5 million, in order to pay off taxes, legal fees, and a number of failed business ventures.

He plans to spend his life as an ex-winner pursuing lawsuits he has filed against police, judges, and lawyers who he says conspired to take his money. "I'm just going to stay at home and mind my p's and q's," he said. "Money draws flies."

(Gambling, Money)

Dates used:_____

J eff Ferrera of Waukegan, Illinois, was reconciling his checkbook and called First National Bank of Chicago to get his current balance.

"Your primary checking account currently has a balance of $924,844,204.32," droned the electronic voice. Ferrera was one of 826 customers who were almost billionaires for a day because of the biggest error in the history of U.S. banking. The goof amounted to almost $764 billion, more than six times the total assets of First Chicago NBD Corporation.

"I had a lot of people saying in jest to transfer it to the Cayman Islands and run for it," Ferrera said. But, like most of the others, he simply reported the error to bank officials, who could say only that it was a "computer programming error."

It pays to remember that all earthly wealth is just as temporal.

—*Chicago Tribune* (5/18/96)
(Heaven, Honesty)

Dates used:_____

In Bill Moyers's book *A World of Ideas II,* Jacob
Needleman remembers:

I was an observer at the launch of Apollo 17 in
1975. It was a night launch, and there were hundreds
of cynical reporters all over the lawn, drinking beer,
wisecracking, and waiting for this 35-story-high
rocket.

The countdown came, and then the launch. The
first thing you see is this extraordinary orange light,
which is just at the limit of what you can bear to
look at. Everything is illuminated with this light.
Then comes this thing slowly rising up in total
silence, because it takes a few seconds for the sound
to come across. You hear a "WHOOOOOSH! HHHH-
MMMM!" It enters right into you.

You can practically hear jaws dropping. The sense
of wonder fills everyone in the whole place, as this
thing goes up and up. The first stage ignites this
beautiful blue flame. It becomes like a star, but you
realize there are humans on it. And then there's total
silence.

People just get up quietly, helping each other.
They're kind. They open doors. They look at one
another, speaking quietly and interestedly. These were
suddenly moral people because the sense of wonder,
the experience of wonder, had made them moral.

*When we have a sense of wonder toward God, we
too have our lives changed for the better.*

—Alan W. Steier
(Kindness, Worship)

Dates used:_____

Worship

In his book *Good Morning Merry Sunshine,* Chicago Tribune columnist Bob Greene chronicles his infant daughter's first year of life. When little Amanda began crawling, he records:

This is something I'm having trouble getting used to. I will be in bed reading a book or watching TV. And I will look down at the foot of the bed and there will be Amanda's head staring back at me.

Apparently I've become one of the objects that fascinates her. . . . It's so strange. After months of having to go to her, now she is choosing to come to me. I don't know quite how to react. All I can figure is that she likes the idea of coming in and looking at me. She doesn't expect anything in return. I'll return her gaze and in a few minutes she'll decide she wants to be back in the living room and off she'll crawl again.

The simple pleasure of looking at the one you love is what we enjoy each time we worship God and bask in his presence.

—Greg Asimakoupoulos
(Fatherhood, Love)

Dates used:_____

Index

Bold face indicates major headings
and the pages on which they're found.

Index

Index

Index

Index

Index

Index

Index